Teach Yourself
VISUALLY™
Excel® 2007

Visual

by Nancy C. Muir

BICENTENNIAL
1807
WILEY
2007
BICENTENNIAL

Wiley Publishing, Inc.

Teach Yourself VISUALLY™ Excel® 2007

Published by
Wiley Publishing, Inc.
111 River Street
Hoboken, NJ 07030-5774

Published simultaneously in Canada

Library of Congress Control Number: 2006934807

ISBN-13: 978-0-470-04595-4
ISBN-10: 0-470-04595-7

Manufactured in the United States of America

10 9 8 7 6 5 4 3 2 1

Trademark Acknowledgments

Contact Us

For general information on our other products and services please contact our Customer Care Department within the U.S. at 800-762-2974, outside the U.S. at 317-572-3993 or fax 317-572-4002.

For technical support please visit www.wiley.com/techsupport.

Wiley Publishing, Inc.

Sales

Contact Wiley
at (800) 762-2974 or
fax (317) 572-4002.

Praise for Visual Books

"Like a lot of other people, I understand things best when I see them visually. Your books really make learning easy and life more fun."

John T. Frey (Cadillac, MI)

"I have quite a few of your Visual books and have been very pleased with all of them. I love the way the lessons are presented!"

Mary Jane Newman (Yorba Linda, CA)

"I just purchased my third Visual book (my first two are dog-eared now!), and, once again, your product has surpassed my expectations."

Tracey Moore (Memphis, TN)

"I am an avid fan of your Visual books. If I need to learn anything, I just buy one of your books and learn the topic in no time. Wonders! I have even trained my friends to give me Visual books as gifts."

Illona Bergstrom (Aventura, FL)

"Thank you for making it so clear. I appreciate it. I will buy many more Visual books."

J.P. Sangdong (North York, Ontario, Canada)

"I have several books from the Visual series and have always found them to be valuable resources."

Stephen P. Miller (Ballston Spa, NY)

"Thank you for the wonderful books you produce. It wasn't until I was an adult that I discovered how I learn – visually. Nothing compares to Visual books. I love the simple layout. I can just grab a book and use it at my computer, lesson by lesson. And I understand the material! You really know the way I think and learn. Thanks so much!"

Stacey Han (Avondale, AZ)

"I absolutely admire your company's work. Your books are terrific. The format is perfect, especially for visual learners like me. Keep them coming!"

Frederick A. Taylor, Jr. (New Port Richey, FL)

"I have several of your Visual books and they are the best I have ever used."

Stanley Clark (Crawfordville, FL)

"I bought my first Teach Yourself VISUALLY book last month. Wow. Now I want to learn everything in this easy format!"

Tom Vial (New York, NY)

"Thank you, thank you, thank you...for making it so easy for me to break into this high-tech world. I now own four of your books. I recommend them to anyone who is a beginner like myself."

Gay O'Donnell (Calgary, Alberta, Canada)

"I write to extend my thanks and appreciation for your books. They are clear, easy to follow, and straight to the point. Keep up the good work! I bought several of your books and they are just right! No regrets! I will always buy your books because they are the best."

Seward Kollie (Dakar, Senegal)

"Compliments to the chef!! Your books are extraordinary! Or, simply put, extra-ordinary, meaning way above the rest! THANK YOU THANK YOU THANK YOU! I buy them for friends, family, and colleagues."

Christine J. Manfrin (Castle Rock, CO)

"What fantastic teaching books you have produced! Congratulations to you and your staff. You deserve the Nobel Prize in Education in the Software category. Thanks for helping me understand computers."

Bruno Tonon (Melbourne, Australia)

"Over time, I have bought a number of your 'Read Less - Learn More' books. For me, they are THE way to learn anything easily. I learn easiest using your method of teaching."

José A. Mazón (Cuba, NY)

"I am an avid purchaser and reader of the Visual series, and they are the greatest computer books I've seen. The Visual books are perfect for people like myself who enjoy the computer, but want to know how to use it more efficiently. Your books have definitely given me a greater understanding of my computer, and have taught me to use it more effectively. Thank you very much for the hard work, effort, and dedication that you put into this series."

Alex Diaz (Las Vegas, NV)

Credits

Project Editor
Timothy J. Borek

Acquisitions Editor
Jody Lefevere

Product Development Supervisor
Courtney Allen

Copy Editor
Laura Town

Technical Editor
Diane Koers

Editorial Manager
Robyn Siesky

Business Manager
Amy Knies

Manufacturing
Allan Conley
Linda Cook
Paul Gilchrist
Jennifer Guynn

Special Help
Sarah Hellert
Cricket Krengel
Laura Sinise

Book Design
Kathie Rickard

Production Coordinator
Adrienne Martinez

Layout
Jennifer Mayberry
Melanee Prendergast

Screen Artist
Jill Proll

Illustrators
Ronda David-Burroughs
Cheryl Grubbs
Jake Mansfield

Proofreader
Jeannie Smith

Quality Control
Laura Albert
Charles Spencer

Indexer
Johnna VanHoose

Vice President and Executive Group Publisher
Richard Swadley

Vice President and Publisher
Barry Pruett

Composition Director
Debbie Stailey

About the Author

Nancy C. Muir is an award-winning author who has written over 50 books on topics ranging from desktop applications to online safety and distance learning. She has also contributed articles to magazines on topics such as distance learning and home design. Prior to her freelance career, Nancy worked in both the software and publishing industries and has taught technical writing at the university level. She holds a certificate in distance learning design from the University of Washington.

Author's Acknowledgments

Thanks to Jodie LeFevere of Wiley for providing the opportunity to work once again on a Teach Yourself VISUALLY book; to Tim Borek for ably keeping everything on track; and to Diane Koers and Laura Town for making sure all the i's were dotted.

Table of Contents

chapter 3 Entering Data

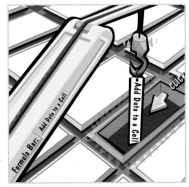

chapter 4 Working with Worksheets

Table of Contents

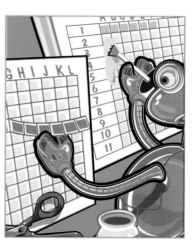

chapter 7 **Formatting Worksheets**

Table of Contents

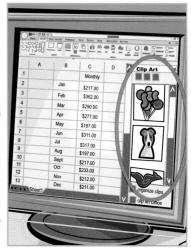

chapter 9 — Previewing and Printing

chapter 10 Communicating Information with Charts

chapter 11 Analyzing Worksheet Data

Table of Contents

chapter 14 Using Excel on the Web

chapter 15 Improving Excel Efficiency

Excel Basics

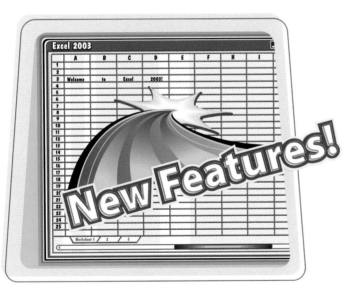

Excel 2003

	A	B	C	D	E	F	H	I
1								
2								
3	Welcome	to	Excel	2003!				
4								

New Features!

Are you new to Excel, or upgrading to the latest version? This chapter shows you how to move around the Excel 2007 program window and work with new features.

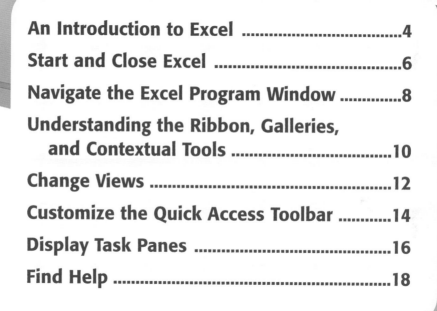

An Introduction to Excel

Microsoft Excel is the most popular spreadsheet program on the market today. You can use Excel to manipulate numeric data like a pro. You can also use the program to track and manage large quantities of data, such as inventories, price lists, expenses and expenditures, and much more. You can even use Excel as a database, entering and sorting records.

Crunch Numbers

Microsoft Excel is best known for its number-crunching features. For example, you can use Excel to quickly tally sales figures, figure averages, and summarize performance numbers for your entire department. You can also use Excel to track your home finances, set up budgets, and forecast future spending. Using Excel's built-in functions, you can perform any kind of mathematical calculation, from the simplest equation to the most complex formula.

Organize Data

Microsoft Excel is also a great tool for organizing data, whether it is a large inventory list for a warehouse of items or simply a small collection of valuables in your home. The row and column format of an Excel spreadsheet is perfect for entering many types of data you need to track. After entering the data, you can perform various sorting operations to control how the data is listed.

Store Data in Worksheets and Workbooks

Data you enter into Excel is stored in a file, called a *workbook*. Excel 2007 workbooks are stored using the .xlsx file extension. Within each workbook, you can store numerous individual *worksheets* to hold your data. You can give your worksheets distinct names, link the data between worksheets, and add and delete worksheets as needed. Learn more about working with workbooks and worksheets in Chapters 2 and 4.

Present Data

You can use Excel's formatting tools to make your spreadsheet data easier to read and interpret. For example, you can add shading to cells, change the number format, or change the font and size of your data. Learn more about formatting worksheets in Chapter 7. You can present your worksheet data to others using charts and graphs. Excel's graphing and charting tools make it easy to turn your data into meaningful visuals, such as pie charts, bar charts, and more. You can learn more about creating charts in Chapter 10.

Share Data

You can share your Excel data with other users, add comments, track changes, e-mail workbooks, and more. You can import data from other sources into your Excel worksheets, or export your data into other file formats. You can also save your data as a PDF, XPS, or HTML file to share with others or post on the Internet. Learn more about sharing Excel data in Chapters 13 and 14.

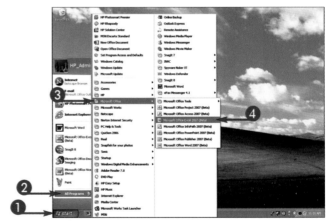

Before you begin working with Excel, you must open the program window. When you finish your work, you can close the window. If you want to save your work, do so before exiting Excel completely.

Start and Close Excel

Start Excel

1 Click **Start**.

2 Click **All Programs**.

3 Click **Microsoft Office**.

4 Click **Microsoft Office Excel 2007**.

The Excel program window opens.

Note: See the section "Navigate the Excel Program Window" to learn how to identify different areas of the program window.

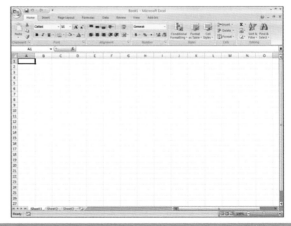

Close Excel

① Click the **Close** icon (⊠).

If this is the only open workbook, both the workbook and Excel will close.

● You can also click the **Office** button (🔘) and then click **Exit Excel**.

If you have not yet saved your work, Excel prompts you to do so before exiting.

② Click **Yes** to save.

The Excel program window closes.

● If you click **No**, the program closes without saving your data.

● If you click **Cancel**, the program window remains open.

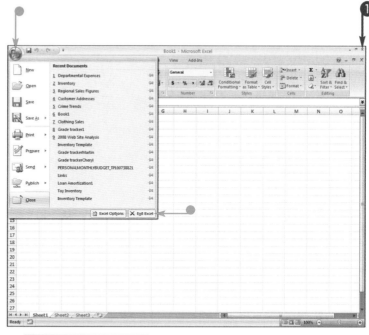

TIP

Can I create a shortcut icon for Excel?

Yes. You can create a shortcut icon that appears on the Windows desktop. Any time you want to open Excel, simply double-click the shortcut icon. Follow these steps:

① Follow steps **1** to **3** in the subsection "Start Excel."

② Right-click **Microsoft Office Excel 2007**.

③ Click **Create Shortcut** in the menu that appears.

● The shortcut appears at the end of the Microsoft Office menu.

④ Click and drag the shortcut to your desktop.

Navigate the Excel Program Window

The Excel 2007 program window displays several common elements found in most Office 2007 programs, including a Office button, the Ribbon, the Quick Access toolbar, and scroll bars. In addition, the Excel window features a Formula bar for entering mathematical formulas. If you are new to Excel 2007, take a moment and familiarize yourself with the on-screen elements.

Microsoft Office Button
Displays the File menu where you find commands to open, save, print, send, and publish files. In addition you can use commands here to close a file or exit Excel, and set Excel options.

Quick Access Toolbar
Displays frequently used features such as Save, Undo/Redo, and Print.

Title Bar
Displays the name of the open workbook file.

Formula Bar
Use this bar to enter and edit formulas and perform calculations on your worksheet data.

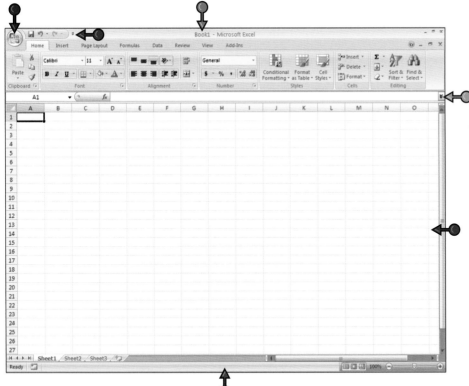

Worksheet
The worksheet consists of rows and columns that intersect to form cells. Cells hold your worksheet data.

Window Frame
Displays status information for the current worksheet or file, as well as view buttons and zoom controls.

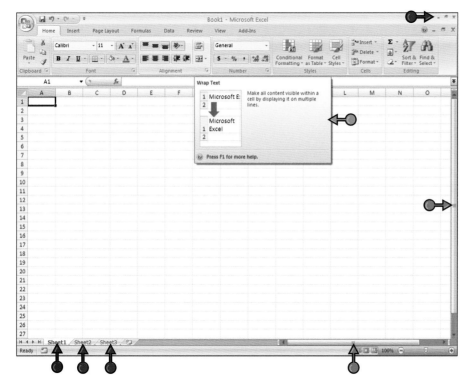

Program Window Controls
Use these three buttons to minimize, maximize, or close the worksheet window.

Super Tooltip
Appears when you place your mouse over a choice on the Ribbon, explaining what a feature does and providing a link to related help information.

Active Worksheet
The active worksheet appears in the Excel work area, and its tab appears highlighted.

Worksheet Tabs
You can use worksheet tabs to view different worksheets in your workbook file.

Vertical and Horizontal Scroll Bars
Scroll vertically or horizontally through a worksheet.

Understanding the Ribbon, Galleries, and Contextual Tools

The Excel 2007 program window has many new tools to help you accomplish your work. The Ribbon replaces toolbars and menus in previous editions of Excel. Galleries of options allow you to preview results of choices before you apply them. Contextual Tools appear when and where you need them.

Change Views

Excel offers different views of your worksheets, depending on what you are currently doing. The Normal view shows one continuous page of columns and rows. The Page Layout view displays your worksheets on individual pages that correspond to printed pages. The Page Break Preview indicates page breaks with lines; you can click and drag these lines to modify where pages break.

Change Views

① Click the **Page Layout View** icon (▣).

● The Page Layout view appears.

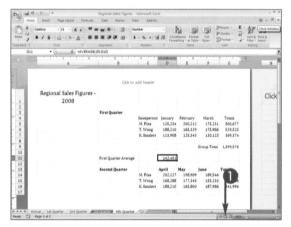

② Click the **Page Break Preview** icon (▣).

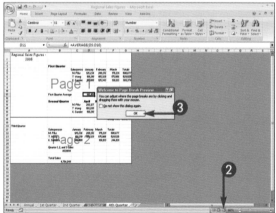

The Welcome to Page Break Preview dialog box appears.

③ Click **OK.**

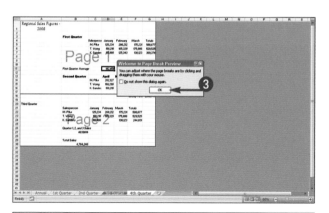

Note: If you do not want to see this dialog box when you enter this view, click Do Not Show This Dialog Again (☐ changes to ☑) before Step 3.

④ Click the **Normal icon** (▦) to return to Normal view.

The Normal view is displayed.

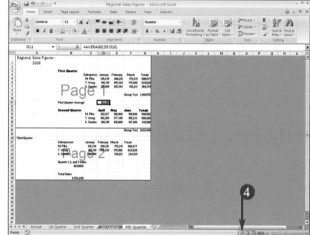

TIPS

Why would I want to use the Page Break view?

You can preview where a printed page will break and move around page breaks before printing by using a click and drag method. See Chapter 9, Previewing and Printing, for more about inserting page breaks.

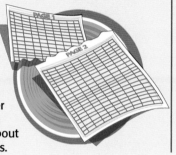

Can I view my Excel worksheet without the various tools showing?

Yes. Click the **View** tab and then click the **Full Screen** button. This removes the Ribbon and title bar from your view. To go back to the regular Excel screen, just press @@Esc or click the Restore Down button in the upper-right corner of the

Customize the Quick Access Toolbar

The Quick Access Toolbar contains four tools by default: Save, Undo, Redo, and QuickPrint. If there are other tools you often use and want immediate access to, for example, the command to create a new file, you can place them on the Quick Access Toolbar.

① Click 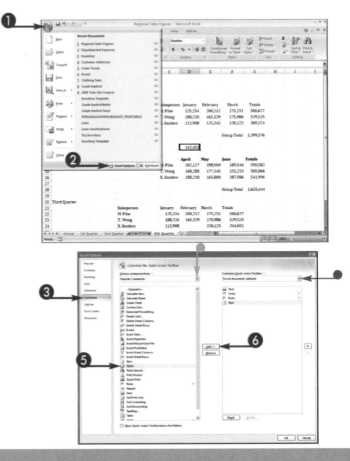.

② Click **Excel Options**.

③ Click **Customization**.

④ Make any of these selections:

● Click here to select the category of commands.

● Click here to specify whether changes are for this document only or for all documents.

⑤ Click a command.

⑥ Click **Add**.

⑦ Repeat steps **4** through **6** to add other commands.

● The commands appear in the list of Quick Access commands.

⑧ Click these arrows to move commands up or down in the list.

⑨ Click **OK** to save your changes.

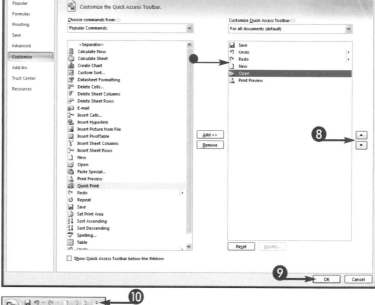

● Click any tool to use a Quick Access command.

Display
Task Panes

Task panes are like onscreen dialog boxes that allow you to search or insert information on specific topics. For example, you can display a Research task pane to search for information on a topic or a Clip Art task pane to search for art in various media. You can close task panes at any time to free up workspace on-screen.

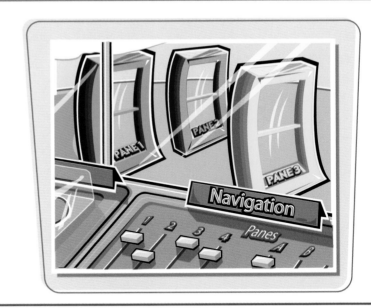

Display Task Panes

Display Panes

1 Click an item in the ribbon that displays a task pane (such as Proofing, Research, or Clip Art).

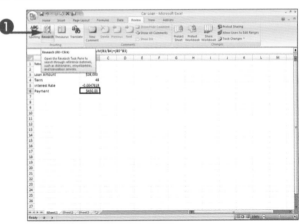

● Excel displays the pane.

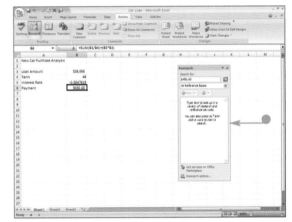

Close the Pane

1 Click ⊠.

The pane closes.

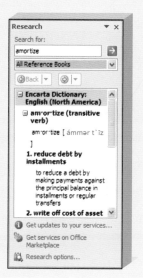

TIP

Can I switch between panes?

In Office 2003, you could use a navigation tool in any task pane to display others. In Excel 2007, navigation tools are not available. You must first click the appropriate tab and then the appropriate tool to display a task pane. Consider task panes to be a variation of a dialog box; clicking a tool on a tab might display a dialog box or a task pane, and either one is easily used to do what you need to do.

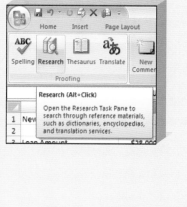

Find Help

You can use the Excel Help tools to assist you when you run into a problem or need more explanation about a particular task. With an Internet connection, you can use Microsoft's online Help files to quickly access information about an Excel feature. The Help window offers tools for searching for topics you want to research.

You must log onto your Internet connection in order to use the online Help files.

Finding Help

① Click the **Help** icon (■).

Note: See the section "Display Task Panes" to learn more about viewing task panes.

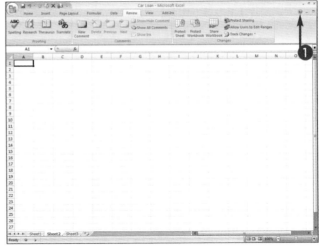

The Excel Help window opens.

② Type a word or phrase you want to research.

③ Click **Search**.

You can also press `Enter` to start the search.

● You can click the **Show Table of Contents** icon (■) to look for topics in the table of contents.

Help displays a list of possible matches.

④ Click a link to learn more about a topic.

The Microsoft Excel Help window opens, and you can read more about the topic.

● You can click links to learn more about a subject.

● You can click the **Back** icon (⬅) and the **Forward** icon (➡) to move back and forth between Help topics.

● You can click the **Print** icon (🖨) to print the information.

⑤ Click ✖ to close the window.

Can I keep the Help window open as I work through a problem?

Yes. To keep the Help window open even as you work within your document, click the **Keep on Top** icon (📌) in the Help window. When you no longer need the window, click ✖.

Workbook Fundamentals

Are you ready to start creating and working with Excel files? This chapter shows you how to work with Excel workbooks, create new files, delete old files, and add password protection to your data.

Start a New Workbook File

Files you create in Excel are called *workbooks*. You can start a new workbook any time you want to create a new file for your Excel data. By default, every new workbook you open automatically contains three blank worksheets you can use to enter Excel data.

To learn more about working with entering data and worksheet structure, see Chapters 3 and 4.

Start a New Workbook File

① Click the **Office** button (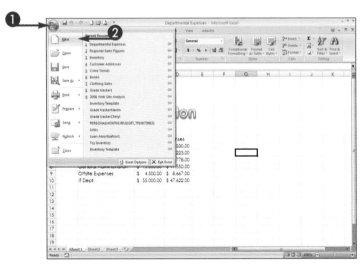).

Note: To learn more about the Office button and tabs on the Ribbon, see Chapter 1.

② Click **New.**

The New Workbook window appears.

You can also press Ctrl + N to create a new workbook.

③ Click **Blank Workbook.**

④ Click **Create.**

Excel opens a new blank workbook containing three worksheets.

Note: To learn how to create Excel templates, see Chapter 15.

You can save your data as a workbook file to reuse it or share it with others. By default, Excel workbooks are saved in the Excel file format, which uses the .xlsx file extension. When you save a workbook, you can specify a folder or drive to save to, as well as a unique filename. After you save a workbook, the new file name appears in the program window's title bar.

Save a Workbook

① Click 📖.

② Click **Save** or **Save As**.

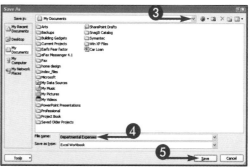

The Save As dialog box opens.

③ Click ▼ to navigate to the folder or drive to which you want to save the file.

④ Type a name for the workbook file.

⑤ Click **Save**.

Excel saves the workbook and the new filename appears on the program window's title bar.

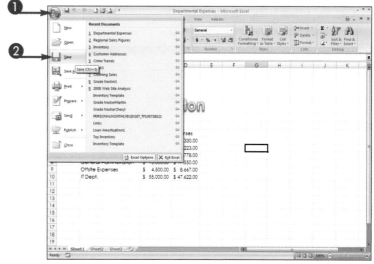

Publish a Workbook as an Excel Binary Workbook File

By default, Excel 2007 files are saved in an XML format. You can spot these formats because file extensions begin with an "x". The Excel Binary Workbook format (.xlsb) is one of the new XML file fomats in Excel 2007. Saving a file in the Binary Workbook format makes the file faster to load and to save. You can read more about various new file formats in the Excel Help system.

Publish a Workbook as an Excel Binary Workbook File

1 Click 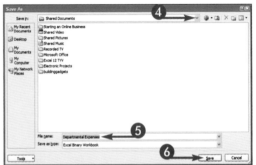.

Note: To learn more about using the Office button and File menu, see Chapter 1.

2 Click the arrow next to Save As.

3 Click **Excel Binary Workbook**.

The Save As dialog box opens.

4 Click here to navigate to the folder or drive in which you want to save the file.

5 Type a name for the workbook file.

6 Click **Save**.

Excel saves the workbook, and the new filename appears on the program window's title bar.

Open an Existing Workbook

You can open a workbook you previously worked on to continue adding or analyzing data. Regardless of whether you store a workbook in a folder on your computer's hard drive or on a disk, such as a DVD, you can easily access files using the Open dialog box.

Excel automatically lists your most recently used workbooks in the File menu.

Open an Existing Workbook

① Click 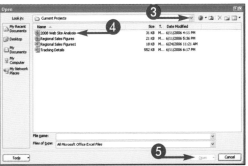.

Note: To learn more about working with the Office button, see Chapter 1.

② Click **Open.**

The Open dialog box appears.

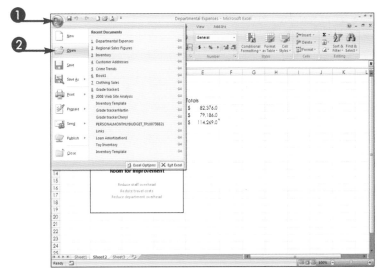

③ Click here to navigate and select the folder or drive where you stored the file.

④ Click the name of the file you want to open.

⑤ Click **Open**.

Excel opens the workbook.

You can close a workbook you are no longer using without closing the entire program window. Closing unnecessary files frees up processing power on your computer.

Close a Workbook

① Click **Close** (✕).

You can also click 🔲 and then ✕.

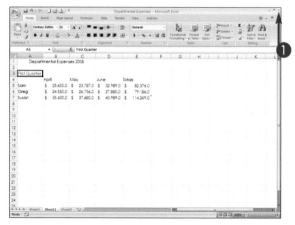

The workbook closes. If this is the only open workbook, Excel closes as well.

Note: To close the Excel program, see Chapter 1.

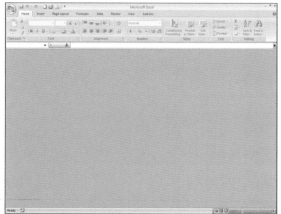

Delete a Workbook

You can permanently remove any workbook you no longer use without exiting the Excel program window. For example, you may want to delete a temporary workbook you created for a quick calculation, or delete old workbooks containing outdated data. You can delete workbooks from the Open or Save As dialog boxes.

Always open and check the workbook prior to removing it to ensure you do not delete a file containing important data.

Delete a Workbook

① Click 📋.

② Click **Open** or **Save As**.

The Open or Save As dialog box appears.

③ Navigate to the Excel file you want to delete and select it.

④ Click the **Delete** icon (⊠).

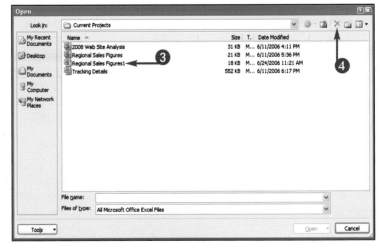

A Confirm File Delete box appears.

⑤ Click **Yes**.

Excel deletes the workbook.

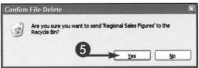

Arrange Workbook Windows

You can open two or more workbooks and view them simultaneously on-screen. For example, you might want to compare data between two workbooks. You can choose from four display modes for viewing two or more workbooks within the Excel program window: tiled, horizontal, vertical, or cascade.

1 Open two or more workbooks.

Note: See the section "Open an Existing Workbook" to learn how to open Excel files.

2 Click **View**.

3 Click **Arrange All**.

The Arrange Windows dialog box appears.

4 Click a display mode (○ changes to ◉).

Tiled arranges the workbooks like mosaic tiles across the screen.

Horizontal arranges the workbooks stacked horizontally.

Vertical arranges the workbooks vertically.

Cascade arranges the workbooks stacked on top of each other in a cascading display.

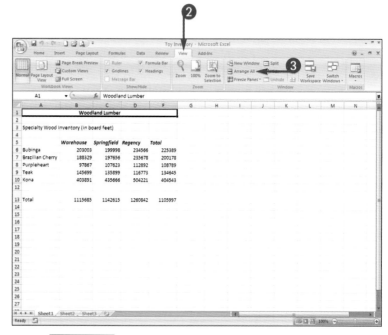

- You can click **Windows of active workbook** (☐ changes to ☑) to display only the sheets in the active workbook.

5 Click **OK**.

This example shows two workbooks arranged horizontally.

- The active workbook's title bar is highlighted.

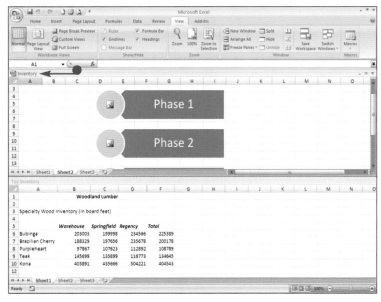

TIPS

How do I return my workbooks to their normal display?

You can click a workbook to make it active, and then click the **Maximize** icon (▢) on the workbook's title bar to return the display to full-screen mode. When you maximize one workbook to full display, all the open workbooks are maximized as well.

Can I compare two sections of a large worksheet side by side?

Yes. You can use the Split feature to help you scroll simultaneously through two parts of a worksheet and view the data in each. To activate the feature, click **View** and then click **Split**. The window divides into four areas. You can then use the two sets of vertical and horizontal scroll bars to move through two different parts of the worksheet.

Protect a Workbook

You can keep people who open your file from making changes to your Excel workbook by assigning a password to it. You can assign a password to a workbook that prevents changes to the number and order of worksheets and preserves the size and arrangement of windows when you next open the file.

The best passwords contain a mix of uppercase and lowercase letters, numbers, and symbols.

Assign a Workbook Password

① Click **Review**.

② Click **Protect Workbook**.

③ Click **Protect Structure and Windows**.

④ Click **Windows** (☐ changes to ☑) to protect the windows in the workbook.

   This selection preserves sizing and display of the windows. The structure of the workbook (number and arrangement of worksheets) is protected by default.

● To allow users to view the file but not make changes, you can type a password (optional).

⑤ Click **OK**.

   If you typed a password in the Protect Workbook dialog box, the Confirm Password dialog box appears.

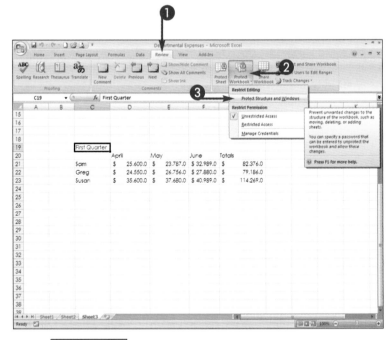

6 Retype the password exactly as you typed it in step **3**.

7 Click **OK**.

Excel assigns the password to the workbook.

Note: To protect cell data, you should use the protect worksheet feature discussed in Chapter 4.

The next time you open the workbook, features for deleting, moving, and renaming worksheets will be unavailable.

Unprotect a Password-Protected Workbook

1 Click **Review.**

2 Click **Protect Workbook.**

The Unprotect Workbook dialog box appears.

3 Type the password.

4 Click **OK.**

You can now make changes to the workbook.

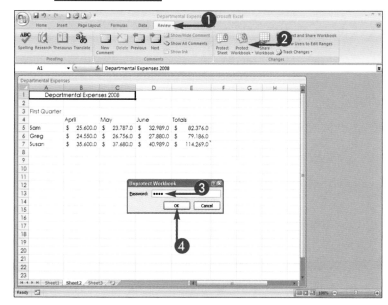

TIPS

What happens if I forget a password?

It is crucial that you remember your Excel passwords. If you lose a password, you can not make changes to the file. Lost passwords cannot be recovered. Consider writing the password down and keeping it in a safe place. Be sure to keep a record of which password goes with which workbook.

How do I remove a password?

To remove a password you no longer want, click **Protect Workbook** on the Review tab, and in the Unprotect Workbook dialog box, enter the current password and click **OK**. You can also reset the password by typing and confirming a new password.

Hide or Show a Worksheet

Sometimes when you are sharing a workbook with others, you might not want them to see every worksheet in it. To keep a worksheet out of view, you can hide it temporarily. When you want to view the worksheet again, you can easily unhide it.

To learn more about protecting workbook structure so that no one can hide or unhide worksheets, see the previous task.

Hide a Worksheet

① Right-click the tab for the worksheet you want to hide.

② Click **Hide.**

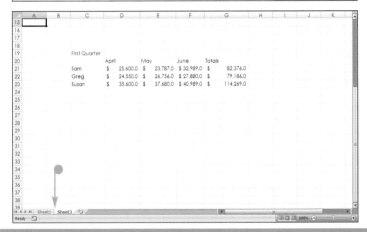

● The worksheet disappears from view.

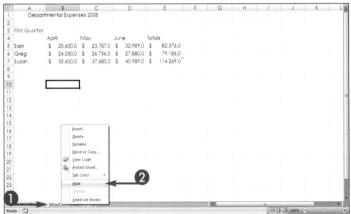

Unhide a Worksheet

1 Right-click the tab area.

2 Click **Unhide.**

The Unhide dialog box appears.

3 Click the worksheet you want to unhide.

4 Click **OK.**

The worksheet reappears.

Note: *If you have protected the workbook structure (see previous task), Hide and Unhide commands are not available.*

TIPS

How do I know if there are hidden worksheets in my workbook?

The easiest way to determine if a workbook contains hidden worksheets is to right-click on tabs for worksheets that are showing. If the command Unhide is listed on any of them, a hidden worksheet is lurking in your workbook!

Can I hide just one column or row in my worksheet?

Yes. If you do not want to hide an entire worksheet but just one portion of it, you can hide any number or rows or columns you like and unhide them when you need them. See Chapter 6 to learn more about hiding and unhiding columns and rows.

Entering Data

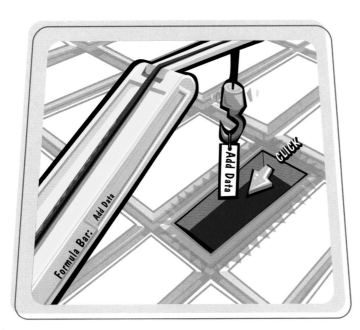

Excel worksheets can hold all kinds of data, ranging from numbers and text to formulas and functions. This chapter shows you various ways to enter data, including several Excel features for speeding up data entry tasks.

You can enter data into any cell within the worksheet. When you click a cell, it immediately becomes the active cell in the worksheet, and any data you type appears within it. You can type data directly into the cell, or you can enter data using the Formula bar.

Data can be text, such as row or column labels, or numbers, which are called *values* in Excel. Formulas are also values. Excel automatically left-aligns text data in a cell and right-aligns values. By default, Excel also considers numerical dates and times that you enter to be values, and assigns right alignment.

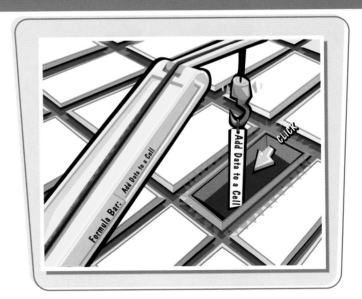

Enter Data

Type into a Cell

① Click the cell you want to use.

The active cell always appears highlighted with a darker border than the other cells.

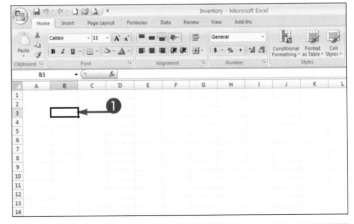

② Type your data.

● The data appears both in the cell and in the Formula bar.

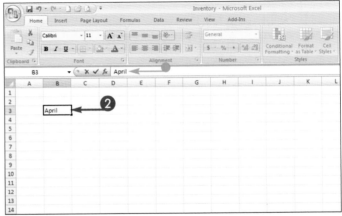

Type Data in the Formula Bar

1 Click the cell you want to use.

2 Click in the Formula bar.

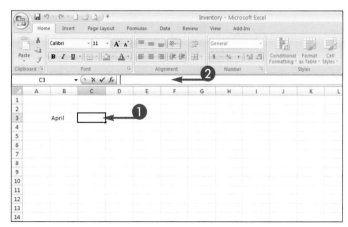

3 Type your data.

The data appears both in the Formula bar and in the cell.

4 Click **Enter** (☑) to accept the entry or press Enter, which accepts the entry and moves your cursor down one cell.

● To cancel an entry, click **Cancel** (☒).

Excel enters the data into your worksheet.

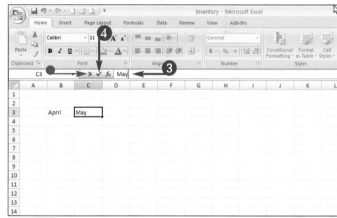

TIPS

What if the data I type is too long to fit in my cell?

Long text entries appear truncated when you enter data into adjoining cells. You can remedy this by resizing the column to fit the data, or by turning on the cell's text wrap feature, which wraps the text to fit in the cell so that the text remains visible. Text wrapping causes the cell height to increase. To learn how to resize columns, see the section "Resize Columns and Rows." To learn how to turn on the text wrap feature, see the next section.

When I start typing in a cell, Excel tries to fill in the text for me. Why?

Excel's AutoComplete feature is automatic. If you repeat an entry from anywhere in the same column or row, AutoComplete attempts to complete the entry for you based on the first few letters you type. If the AutoComplete entry is correct, press Enter and Excel fills in the text for you. If not, just keep typing the text you want to insert in the cell. The AutoComplete feature is just one of many Excel tools to help speed up your data entry tasks.

Turn On Text Wrapping

By default, long lines of text you enter into a cell remain on one line. You can turn on the cell's text wrapping option to make text wrap to the next line and fit into the cell without truncating the text. Text wrapping makes the row size taller to fit the number of lines that wrap.

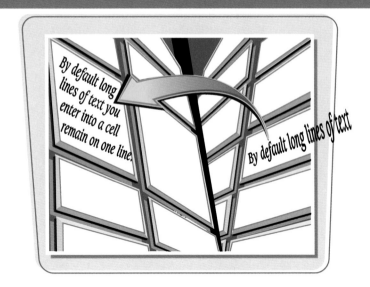

1 Click the cell you want to edit.

Note: You can also apply text wrapping to multiple cells. See the section "Select Cells" to learn how to select multiple cells for a task.

2 Click the **Home** tab.

3 Click the **Wrap Text** icon (⊞).

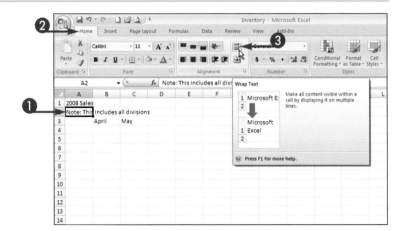

● Excel applies text wrapping to the cell.

Note: See the section "Resize Columns and Rows" to learn how to adjust cell height and width to accommodate your text.

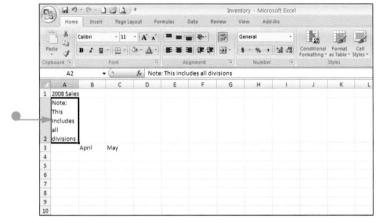

You can resize your worksheet's columns and rows to accommodate text or make the worksheet more aesthetically appealing.

Resize Columns and Rows

① Position the mouse pointer (↖) over the border of the column or row you want to resize.

↖ becomes ↕ or ↔.

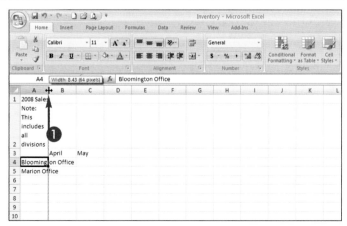

② Click and drag the border to the desired size.

● A dotted line marks the new border of the column or row as you drag.

③ Release the mouse button, and the column or row is resized.

● You can also double-click the right border of a column to quickly activate the AutoFit command.

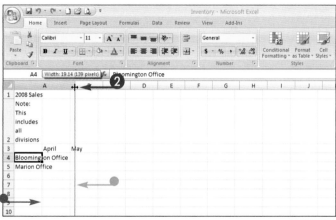

Select Cells

You can select cells in Excel to perform editing, calculating, and formatting tasks. Selecting a single cell is quite simple: You just click the cell. To select a group of cells, called a *range*, you can use your mouse or keyboard. For example, you can apply formatting to a range of cells rather than format each cell individually.

You can learn more about working with ranges in Chapter 5.

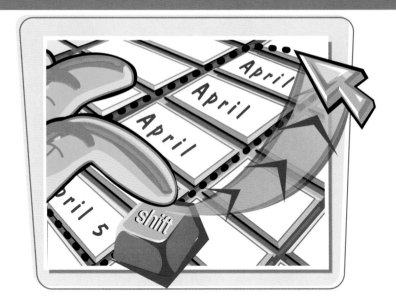

Select a Range

1 Click the first cell in the range of cells you want to select.

2 Drag across the cells you want to include in the range.

▷ becomes ⊹.

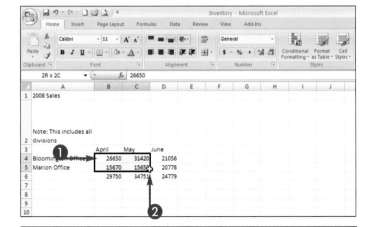

3 Release the mouse button.

● The cells are selected.

● To select all the cells in the worksheet, click here.

You can select multiple noncontiguous cells by pressing and holding Ctrl while clicking cells.

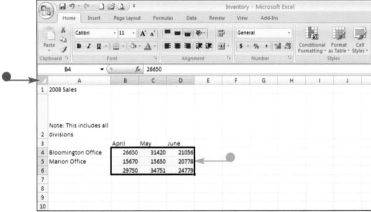

Select a Column or Row

1 Position ⟡ over the header of the column or row you want to select.

⟡ becomes **⬇**.

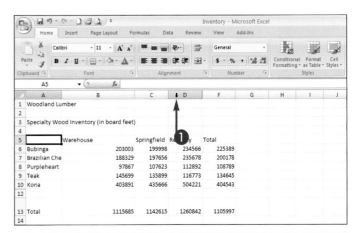

2 Click the column or row.

Excel selects the entire column or row.

To select multiple columns or rows, drag across the column or row headings.

You can select multiple noncontiguous columns or rows by pressing and holding `Ctrl` while clicking column or row headings.

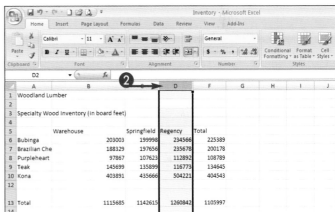

How do I select data inside a cell?

To select a word or number inside a cell, select the cell, and then in the Formula bar click in front of the text; then drag over the characters or numbers you want to select. You can also double-click a word in the Formula bar to select the entire word.

How do I use my keyboard to select cells?

You can use the arrow keys to navigate to the first cell in the range. Next, press and hold `Shift` while using an arrow key to select the range, such as **⬇** and **➡**. Excel selects any cells you move over using the keyboard navigation keys.

Enter Data with AutoFill

You can use Excel's AutoFill feature to help you automate data-entry tasks. You can use AutoFill to add duplicate entries or a data series to your worksheet cells, such as labels for Monday, Tuesday, Wednesday, and so on. You can create your own custom data lists as well as use built-in lists of common entries, such as days of the week, months, and number series.

When you make a cell active in the worksheet, a small fill handle appears in the lower-right corner of the selector. You can use the fill handle to create an AutoFill series.

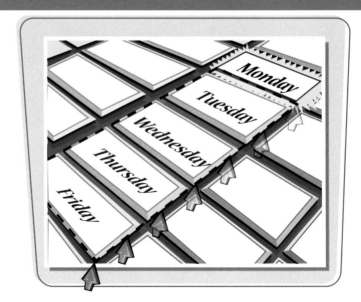

Enter Data with AutoFill

AutoFill a Text Series

① Type the first entry in the text series.

② Click and drag the cell's fill handle across or down the number of cells you want to fill.

You can also use AutoFill to copy the same text to every cell you drag over if the text is not part of a commonly used set, such as the months of the year.

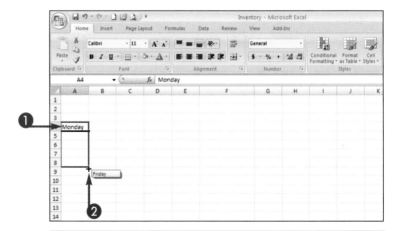

③ Release the mouse button.

● AutoFill fills in the text series.

● An AutoFill Smart Tag (⊞) might appear offering additional options you can assign to the data.

Note: *See the section "Work with Smart Tags" to learn more about smart tags.*

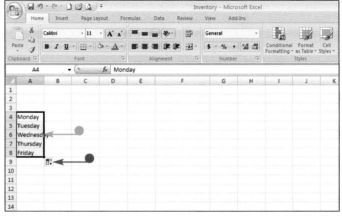

AutoFill a Number Series

1 Type the first entry in the number series.

2 In an adjacent cell, type the next entry in the number series.

3 Select both cells.

Note: *See the section "Select Cells" to learn more.*

4 Click and drag the fill handle across or down the number of cells you want to fill.

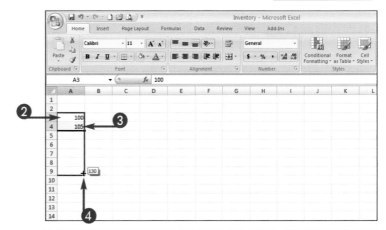

5 Release the mouse button.

● AutoFill fills in the number series.

● A smartag ☐ might appear offering additional options you can assign to the data.

Note: *See the section "Work with Smart Tags" to learn more about Smart Tags.*

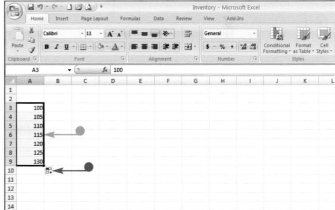

 TIPS

How do I create a custom list?

To add your own custom list to AutoFill's list library, first create the custom list in your worksheet cells. Then follow these steps:

1 Select the cells containing the list you want to save.

2 Click the **Microsoft Office** button (☐).

The File menu appears.

3 Click **Excel Options**.

4 Click **Popular**.

5 Click **Edit Custom Lists**.

The Custom Lists dialog box appears.

6 Click **Import**.

7 Click **OK**.

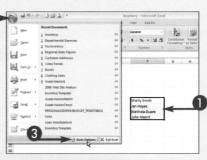

You can use the AutoCorrect feature to quickly correct text you commonly misspell. For example, if you continually misspell the word "autumn" as "autumm," you can add the word to the AutoCorrect dictionary. The next time you mistype the word, AutoCorrect fixes your mistake for you.

You might have already noticed this feature automatically corrects your text as you type in a worksheet. AutoCorrect comes with a list of preset misspellings; however, the list is not comprehensive. To speed up your own text entry tasks, consider adding your own problem words to the list.

Work with AutoCorrect

Add a Misspelling

1 Click [icon].

2 Click **Excel Options**.

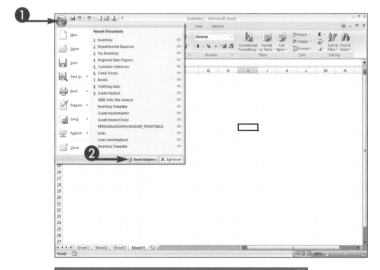

The Excel Options window appears.

3 Click **Proofing**.

4 Click **AutoCorrect Options**.

The AutoCorrect dialog box opens with the AutoCorrect tab displayed.

⑤ Type the common misspelling exactly as you usually misspell it.

⑥ Type the correct or preferred spelling.

⑦ Click **Add**.

AutoCorrect adds the word to the list.

You can repeat steps **5** to **7** to add more words to the list, as needed.

⑧ Click **OK** to exit the dialog box.

⑨ Click **OK** to close the Excel Options window.

Using AutoCorrect

① Click in the worksheet and type the word you commonly misspell.

When you press Enter after typing the word, AutoCorrect fixes the mistake.

Note: If you type something you do not want corrected, press Ctrl + Z to undo AutoCorrect before you continue typing.

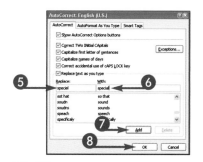

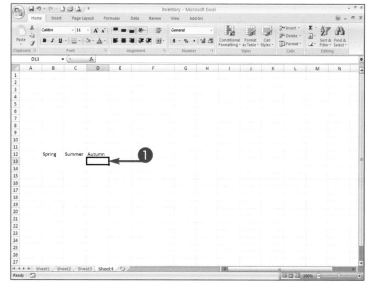

TIPS

How do I remove or edit a word from the AutoCorrect list?

Open the AutoCorrect dialog box to the AutoCorrect tab. Click the word you want to remove and click **Delete**. To edit a word, select it from the list and make your change to the Replace or With text boxes. Click **OK** to exit the dialog box and apply your changes.

Can I customize the AutoCorrect feature?

Yes. You can select or deselect options for AutoCorrect to fix, such as avoiding two initial caps or capitalizing the first letter of a sentence. To control any of the AutoCorrect options, you must first open the AutoCorrect dialog box; click **File**, Excel Options, Proofing, and then **AutoCorrect Options**. Make any changes to the options. You can also turn AutoCorrect off by deselecting the **Replace text as you type** option (☑ changes to ☐). Click **OK** to exit the dialog box and apply your changes.

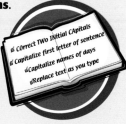

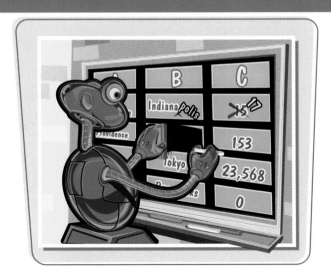

You can perform editing tasks to the data in your worksheets. For example, you might want to change the number values you entered, or add additional text to a cell.

Edit Data

1 Double-click the cell containing the data you want to edit.

● You can also edit the data in the selected cell by making changes to the data as it appears in the Formula bar.

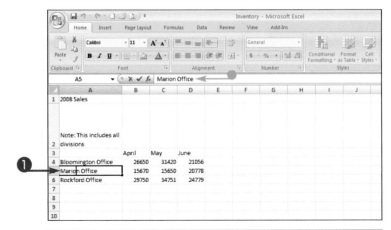

● You can use **Backspace** or **Delete** to remove characters and make corrections to data entries.

You can select data and type over it to replace it with new text.

Note: See Chapter 6 to learn how to rearrange worksheet data. See Chapter 7 to learn how to format data.

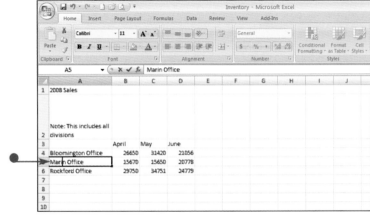

Work with Smart Tags

You can use Excel's Smart Tags to help you save time in your work. Smart Tags are icons that appear when Excel recognizes data and associates it with a task. Depending on the data, Excel might display Smart Tags for AutoCorrect options, paste options, and AutoFill options. For example, when you type a person's name, a Smart Tag might provide a command to add the name to the Office Outlook contact folder.

Work with Smart Tags

① To view a Smart Tag, click [icon].

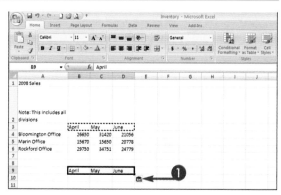

A menu of actions you can perform with the data displays.

② Click an item from the list to perform an action.

To ignore the Smart Tag, continue working with your worksheet data.

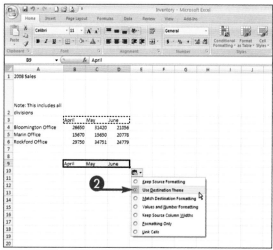

Check Spelling in a Worksheet

You can use Excel's spelling check feature to check your worksheets for spelling errors. Although the spelling check feature is helpful, it is never a substitute for good proofreading. The spelling check feature can catch some errors, but not all, so take time to read over your worksheet for misspellings.

When you start the spelling check feature, Excel checks the entire worksheet, unless you select a specific cell or range of cells.

Check Spelling in a Worksheet

① Click the **Review** tab .

② Click the **Spelling** icon (ABC).

To check only a section of your worksheet, select the cells before activating the spelling check.

You can also press F7 to initiate spelling check.

Excel searches the worksheet for any mistakes, and displays the Spelling dialog box if it finds an error.

● The spelling checker makes suggestions for correct spellings here.

③ Click **Change** to make a correction.

● To correct all the misspellings of the same word, click **Change All**.

The spelling checker moves on to the next error.

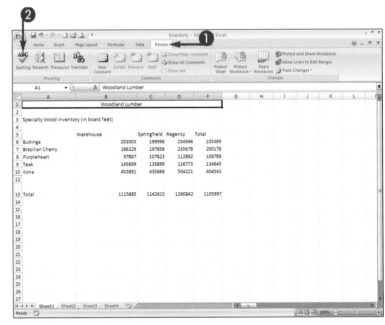

- To ignore the error one time, click **Ignore Once**.

- To ignore every occurrence, click **Ignore All**.

- To add the word to the built-in dictionary, click **Add to Dictionary**.

- To add the word to AutoCorrect's list of common misspellings, click **AutoCorrect**.

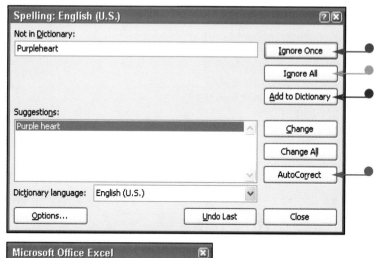

When the spelling check is complete, a prompt box appears.

4 Click **OK**.

TIPS

I added a word to the dictionary, but Excel still marks it as a misspelling. Why?

You might need to enter the word with mixed uppercase and lowercase letters to match the ways in which you plan to use the word. If you save the various formats of the word in the custom dictionary, the spelling check feature recognizes all versions of the word. Also, make sure you add the word to the current custom dictionary and not another dictionary you installed.

Allocate *Upper and*
allocate *Lower case*

Besides spelling check, what other helpful tools can I use to improve my worksheets?

You can use the Research task pane (click the **Review** tab and then click **Research** to display this) to access language dictionaries, a thesaurus, and various online reference sites. To use all the reference resources, you need to connect to the Internet before accessing the Research pane. To learn more about viewing task panes, see Chapter 1.

RESEARCH PANE

CHAPTER

4

Working with Worksheets

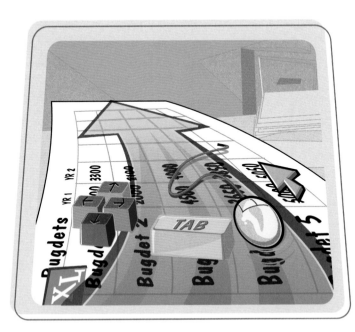

Worksheets are where all the action takes place in Excel. You use worksheets to enter and edit data, perform calculations, and more. This chapter shows you how to navigate around your worksheets and perform various tasks with the sheets.

Understanding Worksheet Structure

Data you type into Excel is entered into worksheets, also called *sheets*. Whether you use a single worksheet or a large collection of sheets, every worksheet is structured in the same way. Before you begin entering text and numbers into your worksheets, it helps to understand how Excel worksheets come together.

Columns and Rows

Worksheets are formatted as a grid formed by columns and rows. Each worksheet has 16,384 columns and 1,048,576 rows. Every column and row has a unique identifier. Columns are labeled by letters arranged alphabetically, and rows are numbered.

Cells and Cell Addresses

Every intersection of a column and a row creates a *cell*. Cells are the receptacles for your Excel data. Every cell has a unique name, also called an *address* or *cell reference*, in the Excel worksheet. Cell names consist of the column and row number, with the column always listed first. For example, cell A1 is the first cell in the worksheet. The next cell to the right is B1.

Active Cell

The active cell in a worksheet is always surrounded by a highlighted border, called the *selector*. The Name box, located on the far left side of the Formula bar, always displays the name of the current cell.

Cell Ranges

As you work with data in a worksheet, you can group related data into a range. A *range* is simply a group of related cells that you can connect. A range can also be a single cell or an entire worksheet. By grouping cells into a range, you can apply formatting or printing to the entire collection, or move or copy the range data at once. Ranges are particularly useful when you begin creating formulas that reference groups of cells.

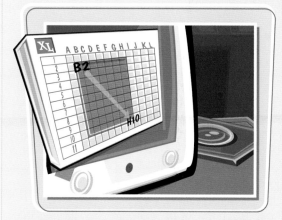

Worksheet Tabs

By default, every Excel workbook starts out with three worksheets. Each worksheet is identified by a tab at the bottom of the sheet. The active worksheet always appears at the top of the stack. You can add more or less worksheets as needed using the Insert Worksheet tab to the right of the three worksheet tabs. You can also give your worksheets unique names to better identify their content.

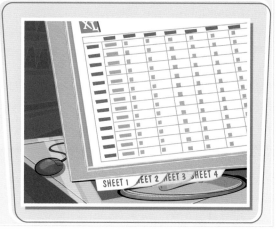

You can use several methods to move around an Excel worksheet. For example, you can move around using your mouse by clicking the cell in which you want to add or edit data. You can also use the keyboard arrows and Tab key to move from cell to cell, or you can utilize a combination of both the mouse and keyboard. You can use the scroll bars to move around a large worksheet.

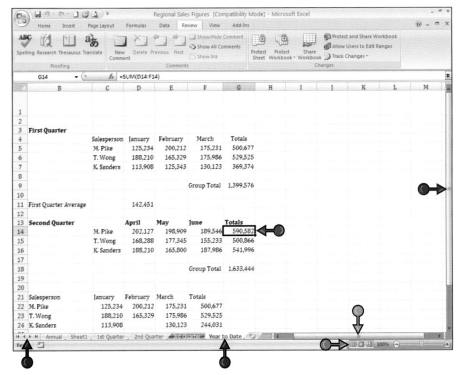

Active Cell
The current cell in which you enter or edit data.

Vertical Scroll Bar
Use to move up and down a worksheet.

Horizontal Scroll Bar
Use to move back and forth horizontally across a worksheet.

Worksheet Navigation Buttons
Use to move among worksheets.

Active Worksheet
The current worksheet. You can click worksheet tabs to make other sheets active.

View Buttons
Use to move among Normal, Page Layout, and Page Break views.

Mouse Navigation

Mouse Action	Action Performed
Click a cell	Selects a cell
Click and drag across cells	Selects any cells you drag across
Double-click a cell	Selects a cell and inserts a cursor ready to enter or edit data
Double-click a cell border	Jumps to the corresponding cell
Click a row number	Selects the entire row
Click a column letter	Selects the entire column
Click and drag row numbers	Selects consecutive rows
Click and drag column letters	Selects consecutive columns
Click in the box at the upper-right corner intersection of the rows and columns	Selects the entire worksheet

Keyboard Navigation

Keyboard Keys	Action Performed
→	Moves right one cell
←	Moves left one cell
↓	Moves down one cell
↑	Moves up one cell
Page down	Moves down one screen
Page up	Moves up one screen
Ctrl + End	Jumps to the lower-right corner of the working area
Ctrl + Home	Jumps to the first cell in the worksheet

Worksheet Navigation Buttons

Worksheet Buttons	Action Performed
⏮	Scrolls to the first sheet in the workbook
◀	Scrolls to the previous sheet
▶	Scrolls to the next sheet
⏭	Scrolls to the last sheet in the workbook

Name a Worksheet

You can name your Excel worksheets to help identify the content. For example, if your workbook contains four sheets, each detailing a different sales quarter, you can give each sheet a unique name, such as Quarter 1, Quarter 2, and so on.

Name a Worksheet

① Double-click the sheet tab you want to rename.

The current name is highlighted.

14		M. Pike	202,127	198,909	189,546	590,582	
15		T. Wong	168,288	177,345	155,233	500,866	
16		K. Sanders	188,210	165,800	187,986	541,996	
17							
18					Group Total	1,633,444	
19							
20							
21	Salesperson	January	February	March	Totals		
22	M. Pike	125,234	200,212	175,231	500,677		
23	T. Wong	188,210	165,329	175,986	529,525		
24	K. Sanders	113,908		130,123	244,031		
25							
26	Quarter 1, 2, and 3 Sales						
27	4639014						
28							

Annual / Sheet1 / 1st Quarter / 2nd Quarter / 3rd Quarter / **Sheet4**

Ready

② Type a new name for the worksheet.

③ Press Enter.

Excel assigns the new worksheet name.

14		M. Pike	202,127	198,909	189,546	590,582	
15		T. Wong	168,288	177,345	155,233	500,866	
16		K. Sanders	188,210	165,800	187,986	541,996	
17							
18					Group Total	1,633,444	
19							
20							
21	Salesperson	January	February	March	Totals		
22	M. Pike	125,234	200,212	175,231	500,677		
23	T. Wong	188,210	165,329	175,986	529,525		
24	K. Sanders	113,908		130,123	244,031		
25							
26	Quarter 1, 2, and 3 Sales						
27	4639014						
28							

Annual / Sheet1 / 1st Quarter / 2nd Quarter / 3rd Quarter / 4th Quarter

Ready

Add a Worksheet

You can add a worksheet to your workbook to create another sheet in which to enter data. By default, every Excel workbook opens with three sheets. You can add more sheets as you need them.

Excel adds a new worksheet immediately after the last worksheet on the right. You can move worksheets to reposition their order; see the section "Move a Worksheet" to learn more.

Add a Worksheet

1 Click the **Insert Worksheet** icon ( ).

A new worksheet appears.

You can click the Home tab, click **Insert** (Insert), and then click **Insert Sheet**.

● Excel adds a new worksheet and a default worksheet name.

Delete a Worksheet

You can delete a worksheet you no longer need in your workbook. Always check the sheet's contents before deleting to avoid removing any important data. After you delete a worksheet, it is permanently removed from the workbook file.

① Right-click the worksheet tab.

② Click **Delete**.

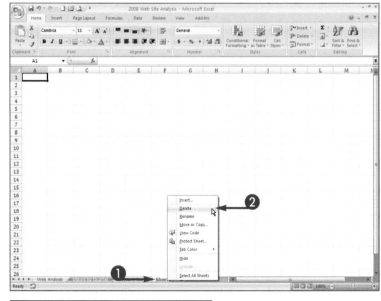

If the worksheet is blank, Excel deletes it immediately.

If the worksheet contains any data, Excel prompts you to confirm the deletion.

③ Click **Delete**.

Excel deletes the worksheet.

Move a Worksheet

You can move a worksheet within a workbook to rearrange the sheet order. For example, you might want to position the sheet you use the most as the first sheet in the workbook.

Move a Worksheet

1 Click the tab of the worksheet you want to move.

2 Drag the tab to move its worksheet to a new position in the list of worksheets.

The mouse pointer ( ) changes to the paper sheet icon ( ).

A small black triangle icon ( ) keeps track of the sheet's location in the group while you drag.

You can also right-click the worksheet tab and click **Move or Copy** to move worksheets with the Move or Copy dialog box.

Note: For more on copying a worksheet without the aid of a dialog box, see the section "Copy a Worksheet."

3 Release the mouse button.

The worksheet is moved.

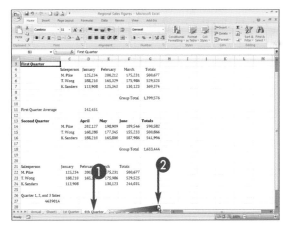

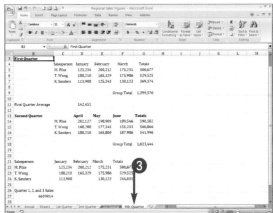

Copy a Worksheet

You can copy a worksheet within a workbook. For example, you might want to copy a sheet to use as a starting point for a worksheet containing new, yet similar, data.

Copy a Worksheet

① Click the worksheet tab you want to copy.

② Press **Ctrl**.

The ⌖ changes to ⌖.

③ Drag ⌖ to a new position in the list of sheets where you want the copy to appear.

▼ keeps track of the sheet's location in the group while you drag.

You can also right-click the sheet tab and click **Move or Copy** to move worksheets with the Move or Copy dialog box.

④ Release the mouse button.

● Excel copies the worksheet as a new sheet in the workbook and gives it a default name.

● Excel labels sheet copies with a (2) after the original sheet name.

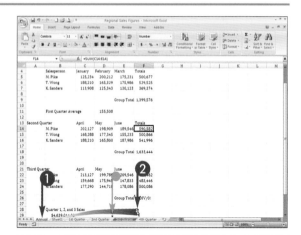

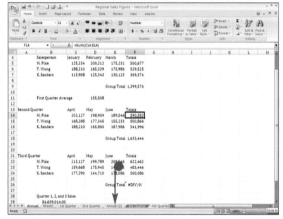

You can add color to your worksheet tabs to help distinguish one sheet from another. The color you add to a tab appears in the background, behind the worksheet tab name. By default, all worksheet tabs are white, but you can assign another color to any tab.

Format Worksheet Tab Color

① Right-click the worksheet tab you want to format.

② Click **Tab Color**.

A pop-up color palette opens.

③ Click a color.

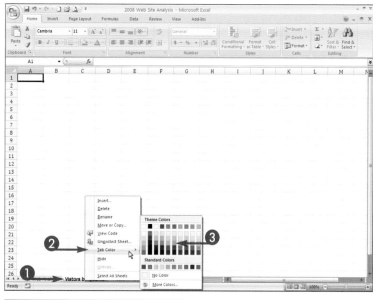

● Excel assigns the color to the tab.

● To see the new tab color, click another worksheet tab.

Setting the tab color to No Color returns it to the default state. If you want to see more color options, click **More Colors** on the Tab Color palette.

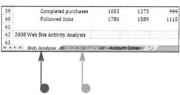

Protect Worksheet Data

You can assign a password to any worksheet within a workbook to protect it from unauthorized use. Essentially, the password locks the worksheet from any changes. Other users can still view the worksheet, but the assigned password protection prevents them from making any changes to the data.

To learn how to assign a password to an entire workbook, see Chapter 2.

To learn how to assign a password to an entire workbook, see Chapter 2.

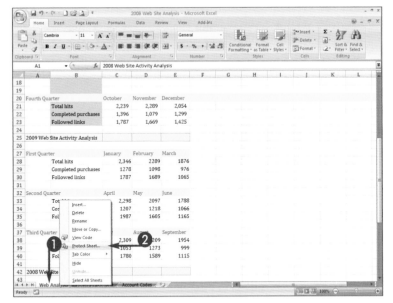

Protect Worksheet Data

① Right-click the sheet tab for the sheet you want to protect.

② Click **Protect Sheet**.

The Protect Sheet dialog box opens.

③ Type a password for the worksheet if you assigned a password.

● You can select which types of changes you want to allow users to make (☐ changes to ☑).

④ Click **OK**.

Excel prompts you to retype the password.

⑤ Retype the password exactly as you typed it in step **3**.

⑥ Click **OK**.

Excel locks the worksheet.

The next time you or another user attempts to make any changes to the worksheet data, Excel displays a warning prompt about the protected data.

TIP

How do I unlock a worksheet?
You can turn off the password protection, thereby unlocking the worksheet. Follow these steps:

① Right-click the sheet tab.

② Click **Unprotect Sheet**.

The Unprotect Sheet dialog box opens.

③ Type the password.

④ Click **OK**.

The worksheet is unlocked. Anyone can now make changes to the data.

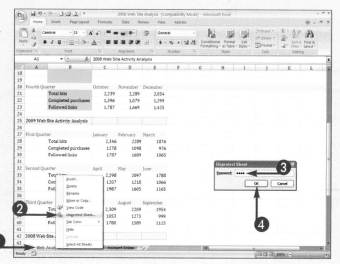

Calculating Data with Formulas and Functions

Formulas and functions are the real driving force of Excel's spreadsheet capabilities. In this chapter, you learn how to build formulas to perform calculations on your worksheet data, as well as tap into Excel's built-in functions.

Understanding Formulas

You can use formulas to perform all kinds of calculations on your Excel data. You can build formulas using mathematical operators, values, and cell references. For example, you can add the contents of a column of monthly sales figures to calculate a total number of sales. If you are new to writing formulas, this section explains all the basics required to build your own formulas in Excel.

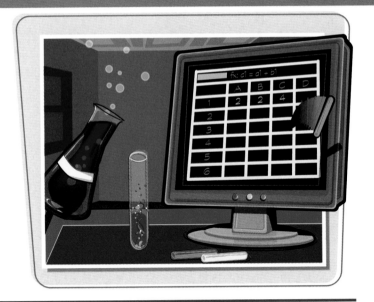

Formula Structure

Ordinarily, when you write a mathematical formula, you write out the values and the operators, followed by an equal sign, such as 2 + 2 =. In Excel, formula structure works a bit differently. All Excel formulas begin with an equal sign (=), such as =2+2. The equal sign immediately tells Excel to recognize any subsequent data as a formula rather than a regular cell entry.

Referencing Cells

Although you can enter specific values in your Excel formulas, you can also easily reference data in specific cells. For example, you can add two cells together or multiply the contents of one cell by a value. Every cell in a worksheet has a unique address, also called a *cell reference.* By default, cells are identified by a specific column letter and row number, so cell D5 identifies the fifth cell down in column D. To help make your worksheets easier to use, you can also assign your own unique names to cells. For example, if a cell contains a figure totaling weekly sales, you might name the cell Sales.

Cell Ranges

A group of related cells in a worksheet is called a *range.* Cell ranges are identified by their anchor points, the upper left corner of the range and the lower right corner of the range. The range reference includes both anchor points separated by a colon. For example, the range name A1:B3 includes cells A1, A2, A3, B1, B2, and B3. You can also assign unique names to your ranges to make it easier to identify their contents. Range names must start with a letter or underscore and can include uppercase and lowercase letters. Spaces are not allowed in range names.

Mathematical Operators

You can use mathematical operators in Excel to build formulas. Basic operators include the following:

Operator	Operation
+	Addition
-	Subtraction
*	Multiplication
/	Division
%	Percentage
^	Exponentiation
=	Equal to
<	Less than
≤	Less than or equal to
>	Greater than
≥	Greater than or equal to
<>	Not equal to

Operator Precedence

Excel performs a series of operations from left to right, which gives some operators precedence over others. When you are creating equations, the order of operations determines the results. For example, if you want to determine the average of values in A2, B2, and C2, and you enter the equation **=A2+B2+C2/3**, you will calculate the wrong answer. This is because Excel divides the value in cell C2 by 3, and then adds that result to the A2+B2. Following operator precedence, division takes precedence over addition. The correct way to type the average formula is **=(A2+B2+C2)/3**. By enclosing the values in parentheses, Excel adds the cell values first before dividing the sum by 3. The following table gives order of operator precedence:

First	All operations enclosed in parentheses
Second	Exponential equations
Third	Multiplication and division
Fourth	Addition and subtraction

Reference Operators

You can use Excel's reference operators to control how a formula groups cells and ranges to perform calculations. For example, if your formula needs to include the cell range D2:D10 and cell E10, you can instruct Excel to evaluate all the data contained in these cells using a reference operator. Your formula might look like this: =SUM(D2:D10,E10).

Operator	Example	Operation
:	=SUM(D3:E12)	Range operator. Evaluates the reference as a single reference, including all the cells in the range from both corners of the reference.
,	=SUM(D3:E12,F3)	Union operator. Evaluates the two references as a single reference.
Spacebar	=SUM(D3:D20 D10:E15)	Intersect operator. Evaluates the cells common to both references.
Spacebar	=SUM(Totals Sales)	Intersect operator. Evaluates the intersecting cell(s) of the column labeled Totals and the row labeled Sales.

Create Formulas

You can write a formula to perform a calculation on data in your worksheet cells. All formulas begin with an equal sign (=) in Excel. You can reference values in cells by entering the cell name, also called a *cell reference*. For example, if you want to add the contents of cells C3 and C4 together, your formula would look like this: =C3+C4.

You can create a formula in the Formula bar at the top of the worksheet. Formula results always appear in the cell in which you assign a formula.

Create Formulas

1 Click the cell to which you want to assign a formula.

2 Type =.

● Excel displays the formula in the Formula bar and in the active cell.

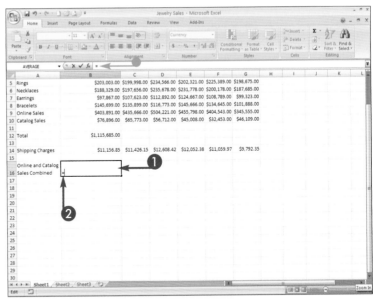

3 Click the first cell you want to reference in the formula.

● Excel inserts the cell reference into the formula.

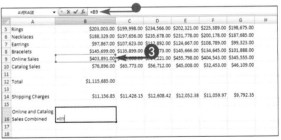

④ Type an operator for the formula.

Note: *See the section "Understanding Formulas" to learn more about mathematical operators.*

⑤ Click the next cell you want to reference in the formula.

Excel inserts the cell reference into the formula.

⑥ Press **Enter** to accept your changes.

● You can also click **Enter** (✓) on the Formula bar to accept changes.

● You can click **Cancel** (✗) to cancel the formula.

● The formula results appear in the cell.

● To view the formula, simply click the cell. The Formula bar displays any formula assigned to the active cell.

Note: *If you change any of the values in the cells referenced in your formula, the formula results automatically update to reflect the changes.*

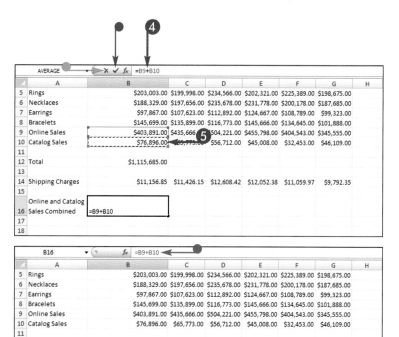

 TIPS

How do I edit a formula?

To edit a formula, simply click the cell containing the formula and make any corrections in the Formula bar. You can also double-click the cell to make edits directly to the formula within the cell rather than the Formula bar. You can use **Backspace** and **Delete** to make changes to the formula and type new values or references as needed. When finished with the edits, press **Enter** or click ✓ on the Formula bar.

What happens if I see an error message in my formula?

If you see an error message, such as #DIV/0!, double-check your formula references, making sure you referenced the correct cells. Also make sure you did not attempt to divide by 0, which always produces an error. To learn more about fixing formula errors, see the section "Audit a Worksheet for Errors" later in this chapter.

Reference Absolute and Relative Cells

By default, Excel treats the cells you include in formulas as relative locations rather than set locations in the worksheet. This is called *relative cell referencing.* For example, when you copy a formula to a new location, the formula automatically adjusts using relative cell addresses. If you want to address a particular cell location no matter where the formula appears, you can assign an *absolute cell reference.* Absolute references are preceded with a $ sign in the formula, such as =$D$2+E2.

Reference Absolute and Relative Cells

Assign Absolute References

1 Click the cell containing the formula you want to change.

2 Select the cell reference.

3 Press `F4`.

Note: *You can also type in the dollar signs to make a reference absolute.*

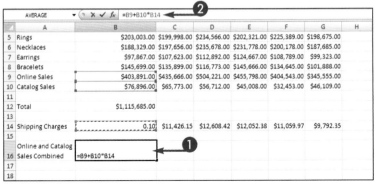

● Excel enters dollar signs ($) before each part of the cell reference, making the cell reference absolute.

Note: *You can continue pressing `F4` to cycle through mixed, relative, and absolute references.*

4 Press `Enter` or click ✓.

Excel assigns the changes to the formula.

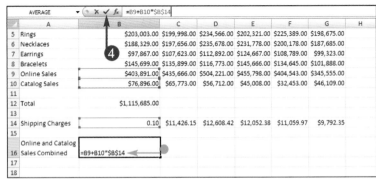

Assign Relative References

1 Click the cell containing the formula you want to change.

2 Select the cell reference.

3 Press F4 to cycle to relative addressing.

Note: You can press F4 multiple times to cycle through mixed, relative, and absolute references.

Note: You can also delete the dollar signs to make a reference relative.

4 Press Enter or click ✓.

● Excel assigns the changes to the formula.

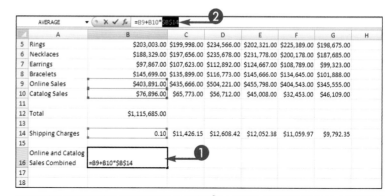

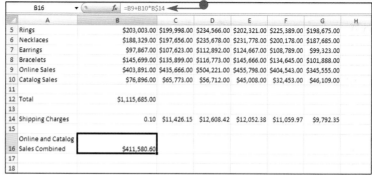

TIPS

When would I use absolute cell references?

You can use absolute referencing to always refer to the same cell in the worksheet. For example, perhaps your worksheet contains several columns of pricing information that refer to one discount rate disclosed in cell G10. When you create a formula based on the discount rate, you want to make sure the formula always refers to cell G10, even if the formula is moved or copied to another cell. By making the reference to cell G10 absolute instead of relative, you can always count on an accurate value for the success of your formula.

When would I use mixed cell references?

You can use mixed referencing to reference different relative cells within the same row or column, such as $C6, which keeps the column from changing but leaves the row relative. If the mixed reference is C$6, the column is relative but the row is absolute. You can press F4 while writing a formula to cycle through absolute, mixed, and relative cell referencing, or you can type in the dollar signs ($) as needed.

Copy
Formulas

You can use Excel's AutoFill feature to quickly copy formulas across rows or columns in your worksheets. If the cell references in a formula are relative, Excel automatically adjusts the formula for the destination cell.

For more on relative and absolute cell referencing, see the section "Reference Absolute and Relative Cells."

Copy Formulas

Copy a Relative Formula

1 Click the cell containing the formula you want to copy.

2 Click and drag the cell's fill handle across or down the number of cells to which you want to copy the formula.

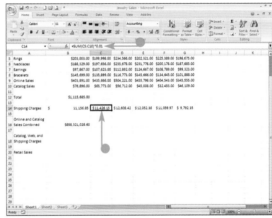

Excel copies the formula into each cell you drag over.

In the case of relative cell referencing, Excel adjusts the formula relative to each cell into which you copy the formula.

● In this example, the copied formula from cell B10 originally referred to cells in column B, but now refers to cells in column C.

Note: See the previous section, "Reference Absolute and Relative Cells," to learn more about cell referencing.

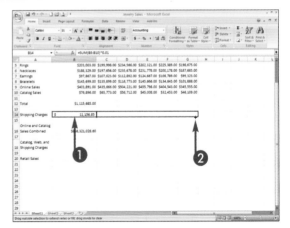

Copy an Absolute Formula

1 Click the cell containing the formula you want to copy.

2 Click and drag the cell's fill handle across or down the number of cells to which you want to copy the formula.

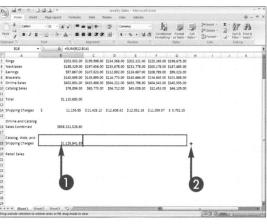

Excel copies the formula into each cell you drag over.

In the case of absolute cell referencing, Excel keeps the absolute cell reference the same regardless of where you copy the formula.

● In this example, the copied formula from cell B16 originally referred to absolute cells in column B, and C14 now references the same absolute cells.

Note: See the section "Reference Absolute and Relative Cells" to learn more about cell referencing.

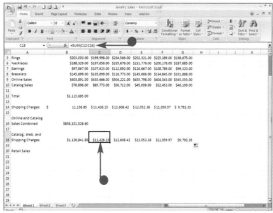

How do I move a formula in my worksheet?

You can move a formula using the Cut and Paste commands on the Edit menu, or you can click the **Cut** ( ) and **Paste** ( ) icons on the Home tab to move a formula in your worksheet. You can also right-click over a selected cell and activate the Cut and Paste commands from the shortcut menu. If the formula's cell references are relative, Excel adjusts the formula for the new cell to which you move the formula. If the formula's cell references are absolute, Excel keeps the cell references the same regardless of the new location in the worksheet.

What does the AutoFill Options smart tag do?

Any time you activate the AutoFill handle of a cell, Excel displays the AutoFill Options smart tag. You can click the tag to view additional options you can apply to the data. For example, you can copy cell contents or formatting. You can choose to ignore the tag and continue working with your worksheet data. The smart tag disappears when you move on to another task. To learn more about Excel's smart tags, see Chapter 3.

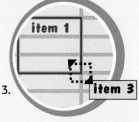

Name Cells and Ranges

You can assign distinctive names to the cells and ranges of cells you work with in a worksheet, making it easier to identify the cell's contents. A *range* is simply a group of related cells, or a range can consist of a single cell. Naming ranges can also help you when deciphering formulas. A range name, such as Sales_Totals, is much easier to recognize than a generic reference, such as B24:C24.

Name Cells and Ranges

Assign a Range Name

1 Click the **Formulas** tab.

2 Select the range you want to name.

3 Click **Name a Range**.

The New Name dialog box appears.

4 Type a name for the range.

5 Click **OK**.

Excel assigns the name to the cells.

Go to a Range

① Click the **Name** ▾.

② Click the range name to which you want to move.

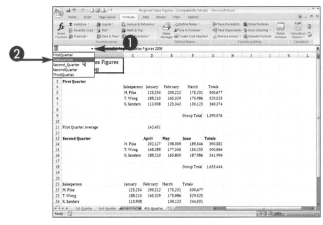

● Excel immediately jumps to the cells.

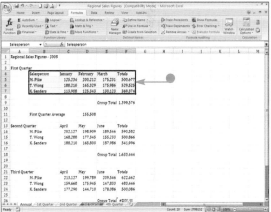

TIPS

Are there any rules for naming ranges?

Yes. Range names must start with a letter or an underscore (_). After that, you can use any character, uppercase or lowercase, or any punctuation or keyboard symbols, with the exception of a hyphen or space. No hyphens or spaces are allowed in range names; instead, substitute a period or underscore.

How do I edit a range name?

You can use the Name Manager to make changes to your range names. On the Formulas tab, click **Name Manager**. Click on the range you want to rename and click **Edit**. In the Edit Name dialog box, enter a new name or change the cells referenced by a range. You can use the Name Manager to edit existing range names or remove ranges you no longer need names assigned to in the worksheet.

Reference Ranges in Formulas

You can reference an entire group of cells in a formula by referencing the range name. This can speed up the time it takes to build a formula in a worksheet, and range names are much easier to remember than the default range names Excel assigns.

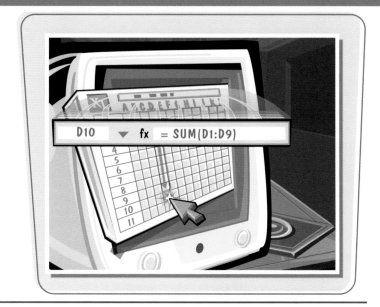

$$D10 \quad \blacktriangledown \quad fx \quad = SUM(D1:D9)$$

Reference Ranges in Formulas

1 Click the **Formulas** tab.

2 Click the cell to which you want to assign a formula.

3 Start or create the formula you want to apply.

Note: See the section "Create Formulas" to learn more.

4 When you are ready to insert a range into the formula, click **Use In Formula**.

5 Click the range name.

Excel automatically inserts the range name.

6 Continue creating the formula as needed.

7 Press Enter.

● You can also click ☑ on the Formula bar to complete the formula.

The formula results appear in the cell.

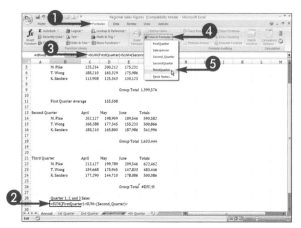

You can reference cells in other worksheets in your Excel formulas. When referencing data from other worksheets, you must specify the sheet name followed by an exclamation mark and the cell address, such as Sheet2!D12. If the sheet has a specific name, such as Sales, you must use the name along with an exclamation mark, followed by the cell or range reference, such as Sales!D12. If the sheet name includes spaces, enclose the reference in single quote marks, such as 'Sales Totals!D12'.

See Chapter 4 to learn more about naming Excel worksheets.

Reference Cells from Other Worksheets

① Click the cell to which you want to assign a formula.

② Create the formula you want to apply.

Note: *See the section "Create Formulas" to learn more.*

③ When you are ready to insert a cell or range from another sheet into the formula, type the sheet name preceded by an exclamation point.

④ Type **!G7**, where *G7* is the cell address or range.

You can continue creating the formula as needed.

⑤ When finished, press **Enter**.

You can also click ✓ on the Formula bar to complete the formula.

● The formula results appear in the cell.

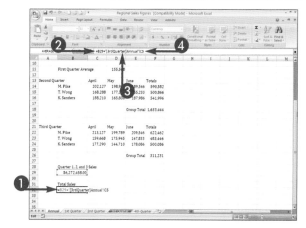

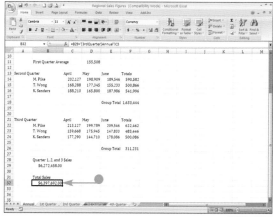

Understanding Functions

If you are looking for a quicker way to enter formulas, you can tap into a wide variety of built-in formulas, called *functions*. Functions are ready-made formulas that perform a series of operations on a specified range of values. Excel offers over 300 functions you can use to perform mathematical calculations on your worksheet data.

Function Elements

Because functions are formulas, all functions must start with an equal sign (=). Functions are also distinct in that each one has a name. For example, the function that sums data is called the SUM function, and the function for averaging values is AVERAGE. You can type functions directly into your worksheet cells or use the Formulas tab of the ribbon. You can also use the Insert Function Wizard or Function Argument dialog boxes to help construct functions. These offer help in selecting and applying functions to your data.

Constructing Arguments

Functions typically use arguments to indicate the cell addresses upon which you want the function to calculate. Arguments are enclosed in parentheses. When applying a function to individual cells in the worksheet, you can use a comma to separate the cell addresses, such as **=SUM(A5,B5,C5)**. When applying a function to a range of cells, you can use a colon to designate the first and last cells in the range, such as **=SUM(B5:E12)**. If your range has a name, you can insert the name, such as **=SUM(Sales)**. See the section "Name Cells and Ranges" to learn more about range names.

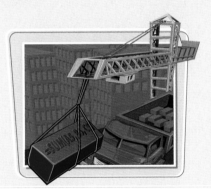

Types of Functions

Excel groups functions into eleven categories, and each category can include a variety of functions:

Category	Description
Cube	If you are using complex OLAP formulas (such as Pivot Tables), cube functions take the OLAP data and display it in a cell.
Date & Time	Includes functions for calculating dates, times, and minutes.
Engineering	This category offers all kinds of functions for engineering calculations.
Financial	Includes functions for calculating and tracking loans, principal, interest, yield, depreciation, and future values.
Information	Includes functions for testing your data.
Logical	Includes functions for logical conjectures, such as `if-then` statements.
Lookup & Reference	Use these functions to locate references or specific values in your worksheets.
Mathematical & Trigonometric	Includes a wide variety of functions for calculations of all types.
Statistical	This category includes functions for calculating averages, probabilities, rankings, trends, and more.
Text	Use these text-based functions to search and replace data and other text tasks.
Database	If you are using Excel as a database program, you can use the database functions to count, add, and file database items.

Common Functions

The table below lists some of the more popular Excel functions you might use with your own spreadsheet work.

Function	Category	Description	Syntax
SUM	Math & Trig	Adds values	=SUM(number1,number2,...)
ROUND	Math & Trig	Rounds a number specified by the number of digits	=ROUND(number,number_digits)
COUNT	Statistical	Returns a count of text or numbers in a range	=COUNT(value1,value2,...)
AVERAGE	Statistical	Averages a series of arguments	=AVERAGE(number1,number2,...)
MIN	Statistical	Returns the smallest value in a series	=MIN(number1,number2,...)
MAX	Statistical	Returns the largest value in a series	=MAX(number1,number2,...)
MEDIAN	Statistical	Returns the middle value in a series	=MEDIAN(number1,number2,...)
PMT	Financial	Finds the periodic payment for a fixed loan	=PMT(interest_rate,number_of_periods, present_value,future_value,type)
RATE	Financial	Returns an interest rate	=RATE(number_of_periods,payment, present_value,future_value,type,guess)
DAYS360	Date & Time	Returns the number of days between two dates using a 360-day calendar	=DAYS360()
IF	Logical	Returns one of two results you specify based on whether the value is TRUE or FALSE	=IF(logical_text,value_if_true,value_if_false)
AND	Logical	Returns TRUE if all the arguments are true, FALSE if any are false	=AND(logical1,logical2,...)
OR	Logical	Returns TRUE if any argument is true and FALSE if all arguments are false	=OR(logical1,logical2,...)

Apply a Function

You can use functions to speed up your Excel calculations. You can use the Insert Function dialog box to look for a particular function from among Excel's eleven function categories.

Apply a Function

① Click the cell to which you want to assign a function.

② Click the **Insert Function** icon (*fx*) on the Formula bar.

● You can also click the **Formulas** tab and click *fx*.

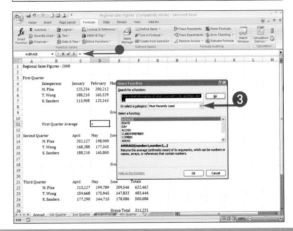

● Excel inserts an equal sign automatically to denote a formula and displays the Insert Function dialog box.

③ Click to select a category.

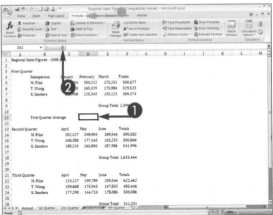

Excel's built-in functions are grouped into ten categories.

Note: *See the previous section, "Understanding Functions," to learn more about function categories.*

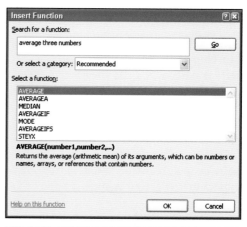

④ Click the function you want to apply.

● A description of the function appears here.

⑤ Click **OK**.

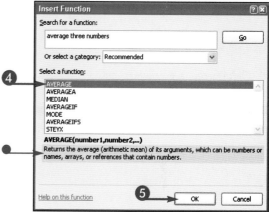

What kind of results can I expect with Excel functions?

Most of the time, the functions you create produce number results. Because functions use different types of arguments, however, some functions produce different types of results:

Result	Description
Number	Number results can include any integer or decimal number.
Time and date	When applying time and date functions, you can expect time and date results.
Logical values	Logical arguments produce results such as TRUE, FALSE, YES, NO, 1, 0.
Text	Any text results always appear surrounded by quotation marks.
Arrays	An array is a column or table of cells that is treated as a single value, and array formulas operate on multiple cells.
Cell references	Some function results display references to other cells rather than actual values.
Error values	If a function uses error values as arguments, the results appear as error values as well. Error values are not the same as error messages.

continued

Apply a Function
(continued)

After selecting a function, you can then apply the function to a cell or range of cells in your worksheet. You can use the Function Arguments dialog box to help you construct all the necessary components of a function. The dialog box can help you determine what values you need to enter to build the formula.

Apply a Function *(continued)*

The Function Arguments dialog box appears.

Note: *You can also go directly to the Function Arguments dialog box for a particular function by clicking a formula category in the Function Library group of the Formulas tab and selecting that function.*

⑥ Depending on the function's arguments, select the desired cells for each argument required by the function.

You can select a cell or range of cells directly in the worksheet, and Excel automatically adds the references to the argument.

You can also type a range or cell address directly in the argument text box.

● The dialog box displays additional information about the function here.

⑦ If needed, continue adding the necessary cell references to complete all of the function's arguments.

⑧ When finished constructing the arguments, click **OK**.

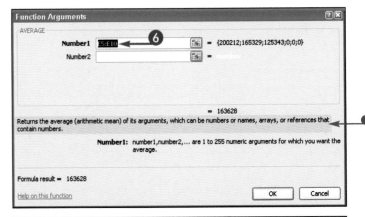

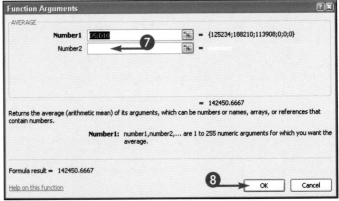

● Excel displays the function results in the cell.

● The function appears in the Formula bar.

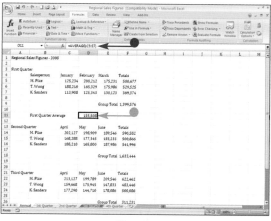

Edit a Function

① Click the cell containing the function you want to edit.

② Click the **Formulas** tab.

③ Click **Insert Function**.

Excel displays the Function Arguments dialog box, and you can make changes to the cell references or values as needed.

④ Click **OK**.

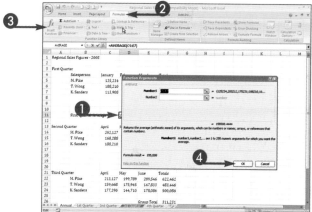

TIPS

How can I find help with a particular function?

If you click **Help on this function** in either the Insert Function or Function Arguments dialog box, you can access Excel's Help files to find out more about the function. The function help includes an example of the function in action and tips about how to use the function.

The Function Arguments dialog box covers up the cells I need to select. How do I move the dialog box out of the way?

You can click the **Collapse** icon (■) at the end of the argument text box to minimize the dialog box. You can then select any cells needed and click the **Expand** icon (■) to maximize the dialog box again. You can also click and drag the dialog box by its title bar to move it around the screen.

Total Cells with AutoSum

One of the most popular functions available in Excel is the AutoSum function. AutoSum automatically totals the contents of cells. For example, you can quickly total a column of sales figures. AutoSum works by guessing which surrounding cells you want to total, or you can specify exactly which cells to sum.

Total Cells with AutoSum

Apply AutoSum

1. Click in the cell where you want to insert a sum total.

2. Click the **Formulas** tab.

3. Click **AutoSum**.

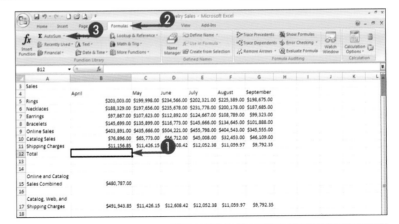

● AutoSum immediately attempts to total the adjacent cells.

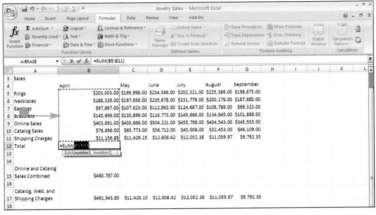

- To sum another range of cells instead of AutoSum's guess, select the cells you want to include in the sum.

4 Press **Enter** or click ✔.

- Excel totals the selected cells.

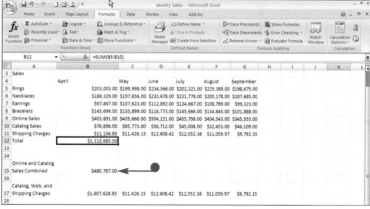

TIPS

Can I total cells without applying a function?

Yes. You can use the AutoCalculate feature to quickly sum cells or apply results from several other popular functions without having to insert a formula or function. You can select a group of cells you want to total, and Excel immediately adds all the cell contents and displays a total, average, and count in the status bar at the bottom of the program window. To change the calculation type, right-click the total on the status bar and click another function. To sum noncontiguous cells, press and hold **Ctrl** while clicking cells.

Can I apply AutoSum to both rows and columns at the same time?

Yes. Simply select both the row and column of data you want to sum, along with a blank row and column to hold the results. When you apply the AutoSum function, Excel sums the row and column and displays the results in the blank row and column.

Check for Formula Errors

If something is wrong with a formula you apply in a worksheet, Excel displays an error message, usually in the cell containing the formula results. Error messages do not always clarify what is wrong with the formula or identify what you need to do to make a correction. The following checklist offers a few practical solutions that can help you determine the nature of the error.

Check Cell References

One of the most common mistakes users make is placing the wrong cell references into a formula. For example, instead of clicking cell C7, you click cell C8. Always double-check the cell references you used in your formula. If you referenced cells from other worksheets, double-check those references to make sure you used the correct sheet name as well as the correct cell references.

Check for Typing Errors

Typing errors can also cause formulas to go awry. Double-check your use of punctuation in your formulas. Remember, you must use colons to designate ranges in your cell references, such as B5:E12, and sometimes a mistyped semicolon can cause an error. If you use named ranges in a formula, spell the range name correctly. If a range name includes a space, be sure to enclose the range name in quotation marks when referencing the range from another worksheet.

Check Cell Data

Always double-check the contents of your referenced cells to make sure the content is not causing the formula error. Excel cannot calculate an answer if you try to divide by zero or use a nonnumeric value in a mathematic formula.

Check Parentheses

Make sure parentheses in a formula appear in the right order. Formulas require a beginning and ending parenthesis for each use, and the parentheses must surround the formula arguments. When nesting arguments, which allows you to use parentheses within parentheses, double-check to make sure your formula includes all the necessary parentheses. If one is missed, a formula error occurs.

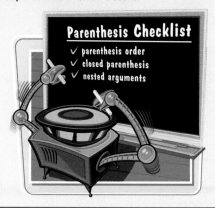

Check Operator Precedence

It is important to remember the rule of operator precedence. Excel tackles mathematical operators in a particular order, as explained in the section "Understanding Formulas." If you experience incorrect formula results, start by checking the order of your formula's operators.

Check Function Arguments

When you use functions, always check for missing arguments. Also remember that when you apply functions, you must use the right data with the right function. Some functions require a certain type of data to perform a calculation. For example, if the function is expecting numeric data and you reference a cell with text data instead, this causes a formula error. Revisit the Function Arguments dialog box for the formula to double-check what data types are required by the function.

Remove Formatting

Some functions do not work well with formatted cell data, such as percent signs rather than plain numbers. If you experience a formula error with a function, try removing any formatting for the referenced cells.

Audit a Worksheet for Errors

When dealing with larger Excel worksheets that require scrolling through many cells, it is not always easy to figure out the source of a formula error. To help with errors that arise, you can use Excel's Formula Auditing group of tools on the Formulas tab of the Ribbon, which includes several tools for examining and correcting formula errors. The Error Checking feature looks through your worksheet for errors and helps you find solutions.

Audit a Worksheet for Errors

Apply Error Checking

① Click the **Formulas** tab.

Excel displays the Formulas tab.

② Click the **Error Checking** icon (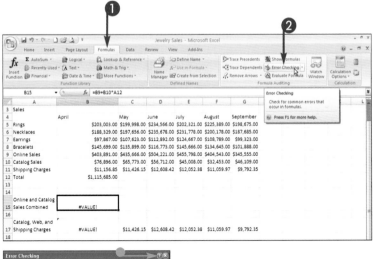).

Excel displays the Error Checking dialog box and highlights the first cell containing an error.

③ To fix the error, click **Edit in Formula Bar**.

● To find help with an error, click here to open the Help files.

● To ignore the error, click **Ignore Error**.

④ Make edits to the cell references in the Formula bar.

⑤ Click **Resume**.

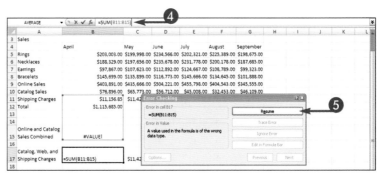

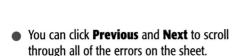

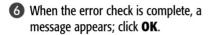

● You can click **Previous** and **Next** to scroll through all of the errors on the sheet.

⑥ When the error check is complete, a message appears; click **OK**.

TIP

What kind of error messages does Excel display for formula errors?

The following table explains the different types of error values that can appear in cells when an error occurs:

Error Message	Problem	Solution
######	The cell is not wide enough to contain the value.	Widen the column width.
#N/A	Value is not available.	Check to make sure the formula references the correct value.
#NAME?	Does not recognize text in a formula.	Make sure the name referenced is correct.
#NUM!	Invalid numeric value.	Check the function for an unacceptable argument.
#REF!	Invalid cell reference.	Correct cell references.
#VALUE!	Wrong type of argument or operand.	Double-check arguments and operands.

continued

Audit a Worksheet for Errors *(continued)*

Auditing tools can trace the path of your formula components and check each cell reference that contributes to the formula. When tracing the relationships between cells, you can display tracer lines to find *precedents*, cells referred to in a formula, or *dependents*, cells that contain the formula results.

Audit A Worksheet For Errors *(continued)*

Trace Precedents

1 Click the cell containing the formula results or content you want to trace.

2 Click the **Formulas** tab.

3 Click **Trace Precedents**.

● To trace dependents instead, click **Trace Dependents**.

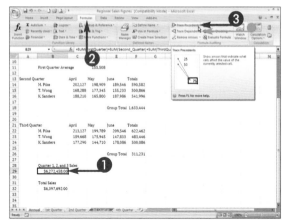

Excel displays trace lines from the current cell to the cells referenced in the formula.

You can make changes to the cell contents or the formula.

● In this example, the trace lines show the three cell ranges that are referenced in the formula.

● You can click **Remove Arrows** to turn off all trace lines.

To turn off just dependent trace lines, click the arrow on the Remove Arrows tool and click **Remove Dependent Arrows**.

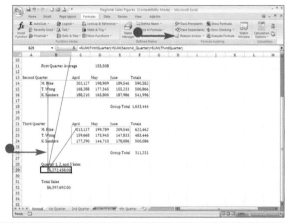

Trace Errors

1 Click the cell containing the error you want to trace.

2 Click the **Formulas** bar.

3 Click .

4 Click **Trace Error**.

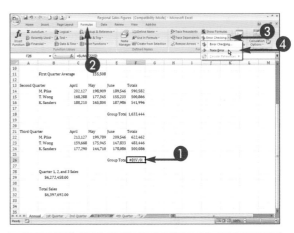

Excel displays trace lines from the current cell to any cells referenced in the formula.

You can make changes to the cell contents or the formula to correct the error.

● In this example, a number is divided by zero.

● You can click **Remove Arrows** to turn off the trace lines.

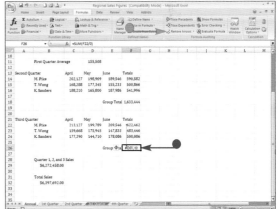

TIPS

How do I use the smart tag to fix formula errors?

Excel displays a smart tag icon any time you encounter an error. You can click the smart tag to view a menu of options, including options for correcting the error. For example, you can click **Help on this error** to find out more about the error message.

What does the Evaluate Formula button do?

You can click the **Evaluate Formula** icon (🔲) in the Formula Auditing group of tools in the Formulas tab to check your formula or function step by step. When you click the cell containing the formula you want to evaluate and then click 🔲, Excel opens the Evaluate Formula dialog box, and you can evaluate each portion of the formula for correct references and values.

Rearranging Worksheet Data

You can rearrange your worksheet data to improve the presentation of your worksheet information. This chapter shows you how to use Excel's many tools to make adjustments to the worksheet structure.

Move and Copy Data

You can use the Cut, Copy, and Paste commands to copy data within Excel, or move and share data between other Office programs. For example, you might cut a row of labels and paste them into another worksheet, or copy a formula from one cell to another cell in the same worksheet. You can also drag and drop data to move and copy it within a worksheet.

The Copy command makes a duplicate of the selected data, and the Cut command removes the data from the original file entirely. Excel places data that you copy or cut in the Windows Clipboard until you are ready to paste it into place.

Move and Copy Data

Move or Copy Data

1 Select the data you want to move or copy.

Note: See Chapter 3 to learn how to select cells.

2 Click **Home**.

3 Click **Cut** (✂) to move data, or click **Copy** (📋) to copy the data.

Note: You can also use the Cut, Copy, and Paste commands to move and copy entire rows or columns.

The data is placed in the Windows Clipboard.

4 Click where you want to insert the data.

You can also open another workbook or worksheet to paste the data.

5 Click **Paste** (📋).

The data appears in the new location.

You can also click the arrow on the Paste button and specify what to paste from the drop-down menu that appears.

A smart tag (📋) might appear when you paste the data. You can click 📋 to view a list of options you can apply to the pasted data.

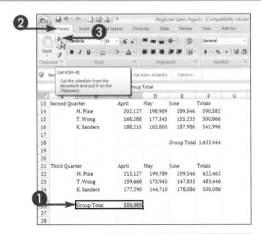

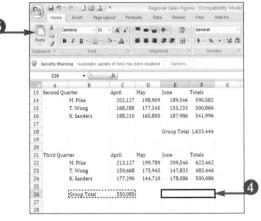

Drag and Drop Data

1 Select the data you want to move or copy.

Note: See Chapter 3 to learn how to select cells.

2 Position the mouse pointer (↖) over the selected cell's border.

↖ changes to ✛ .

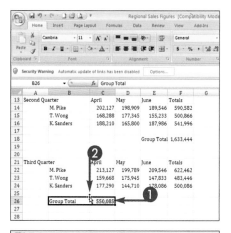

3 Click and drag the data to a new location in the worksheet.

To copy the data, press and hold Ctrl while dragging.

The data appears in the new location.

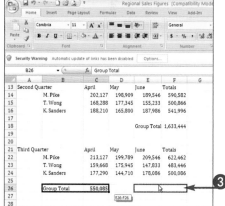

TIPS

When I paste data, an icon appears. What is it?

The Paste Options smart tag (📋) appears when you perform any copy or paste tasks. You can click 📋 to view a drop-down list of related options for the task you are performing. You can click an option from the list to activate the option. If you prefer not to use 📋, you can ignore it. The tag disappears if you continue working on the file.

Can I paste only the results of a formula, and not the formula itself?

Yes. You can use the Paste Values command on the menu that appears when you click **Paste** on the Home tab. Although pasting the formula causes the formula to calculate relative values, pasting the value copies the results of the formula to the selected cell. If the original formula recalculates, the pasted value will not.

Delete Data or Cells

You can delete Excel data you no longer need. When you decide to delete data, you can choose whether you want to remove the data and keep the cell or delete the cell entirely. When you delete a cell's contents, only the data is removed. When you delete a cell, Excel removes the cell as well as its contents. The existing cells in your worksheet shift over or up to fill any gap in the worksheet structure.

Delete Data or Cells

Delete Data

① Click the cell or select the cells containing the data you want to remove.

Note: See Chapter 3 to learn how to select cells.

② Press **Delete**.

Excel deletes the data from the cell.

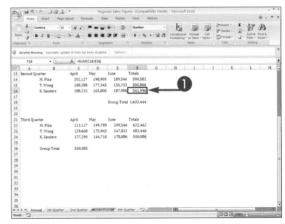

Delete Cells

① Click the cell or select the cells you want to remove.

Note: See Chapter 3 to learn how to select cells.

② Right-click over the cell or range.

③ Click **Delete**.

You can also click **Delete** on the Home tab.

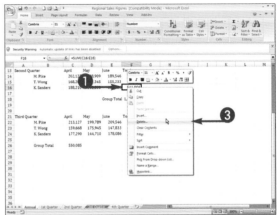

The Delete dialog box opens.

④ Click a deletion option (○ changes to ◉).

You can also open another file to copy to.

⑤ Click **OK**.

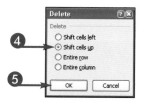

Excel removes the cells and their content from the worksheet.

Other cells shift over or up to fill the void of any cells you remove from a worksheet.

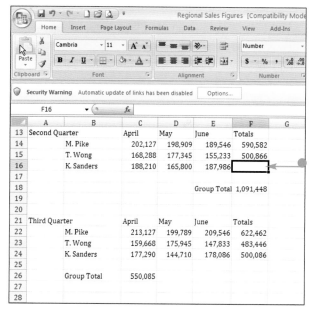

TIP

Can I remove a cell's formatting without removing the content?

Yes. You can.

① Click **Home**.

② Click **Cell Styles**.

③ Click the **Normal** style from the gallery that appears, to clear any cell formatting that has been applied.

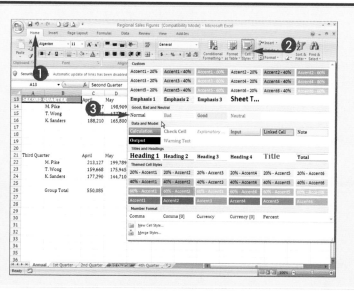

Add Columns and Rows

You can add columns and rows to your worksheets to add more data. For example, you might need to add a column in the middle of several existing columns to add data you left out the first time you created the workbook.

Add Columns and Rows

Add a Column

① Right-click the column to the right of where you want to insert a new column.

Note: See Chapter 3 to learn how to select columns and rows.

② Click **Insert**.

● Excel adds a column.

● You can also click **Insert** on the Home tab to insert a cell, row, column, or worksheet from a drop-down menu.

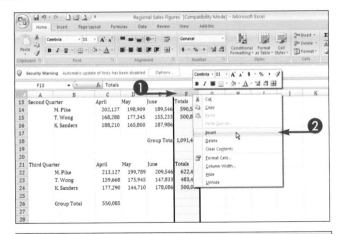

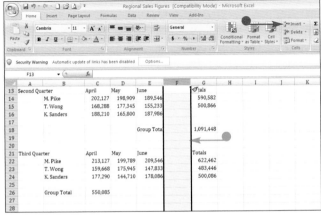

Add a Row

① Right-click the row below where you want to insert a new row.

Note: See Chapter 3 to learn how to select columns and rows.

② Click **Insert**.

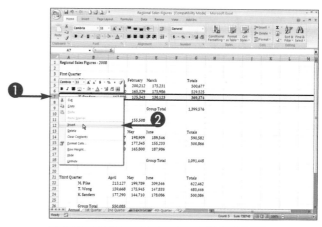

● Excel adds a row.

● You can also click **Insert** on the Home tab to insert a cell, row, column, or worksheet from a drop-down menu.

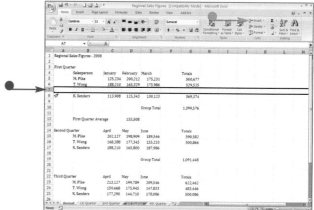

Can I insert a multiple number of columns and rows?

Yes. Select two or more columns or rows in the worksheet, right-click, and choose **Insert**. Excel adds the same number of new columns or rows as the number you originally selected. You can also click **Insert** and click **Insert Sheet Columns** or **Insert Sheet Rows** to insert multiple columns or rows into your worksheet.

What happens to formula calculations when I insert rows or columns?

Absolute cell references change; for example, if your formula added the values in B2 and C3 and you insert a new first column, the formula will now refer to the new B2 and C3 values. Relative cell references will adjust.

Delete Columns and Rows

You can remove columns or rows you no longer need in the worksheet. For example, you might remove a row of out-of-date data. When you delete an entire column or row, Excel deletes any existing data within the selected cells. Excel also moves the other columns and rows to fill the space left by the deletion.

Delete Columns and Rows

Delete a Column

1 Right-click the column you want to delete.

Note: See Chapter 3 to learn how to select columns and rows.

2 Click **Delete**.

Note: If you press Delete *, Excel deletes the column's contents instead of the entire column.*

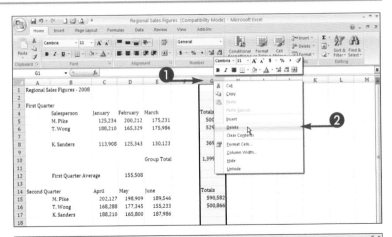

Excel deletes the column.

● You can also click **Delete** on the Home tab to remove a column or row.

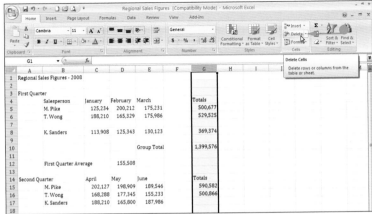

Delete a Row

1 Right-click the row you want to delete.

Note: *See Chapter 3 to learn how to select columns and rows.*

2 Click **Delete**.

Note: *If you press* Delete *, Excel deletes the row's contents instead of the entire row.*

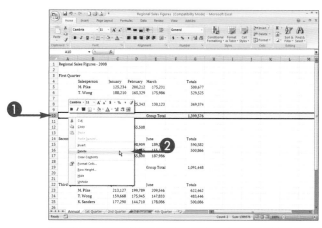

Excel deletes the row.

● You can also click **Delete** on the Home tab to remove a row.

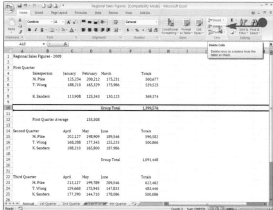

TIPS

How do I delete an entire worksheet from my workbook?	**I accidentally deleted a column I need. How do I reinsert it?**
To remove a worksheet, right-click the worksheet tab and then click **Delete** from the shortcut menu. If the sheet contains any existing data, Excel prompts you to confirm the deletion by clicking **Delete** in a dialog box. To learn more about adding and deleting worksheets from a workbook file, see Chapter 4. 	If you click the **Undo** icon ( ) on the Quick Access toolbar immediately after deleting a row or column, you can undo the action. Excel reinserts the row or column, including any data it contained. You can also press Ctrl + Z to undo the last action.

Center Data across Columns

You can center a title or heading across a range of cells in your worksheet. For example, you might want to include a title across multiple columns of labels. You can use the Merge and Center command to quickly create a merged cell to hold the title text.

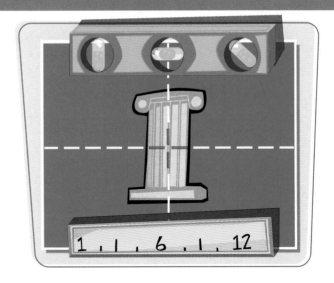

Center Data across Columns

① Select the cell containing the text you want to center and the cells to the right of it across which you want to center that text.

Note: See Chapter 3 to learn how to select columns and rows.

② Click the **Home** tab.

③ Click **Merge and Center** (▦).

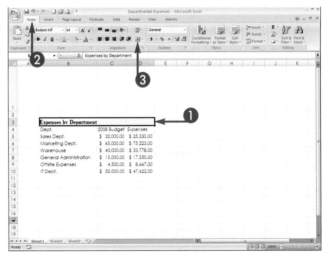

● Excel merges the cells and centers the text.

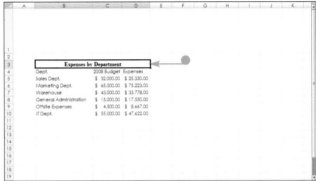

You can quickly turn column labels into row labels or row labels into column labels using the Transpose command. For example, you might create a worksheet to include three column labels and four row labels but later decide it is better the other way around. Rather than retype the text, you can activate the Transpose command.

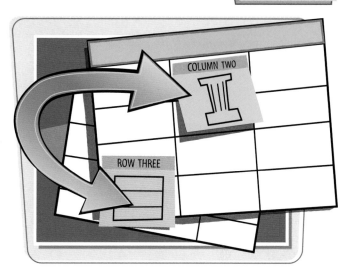

Transpose Columns and Rows

① Select the cells containing the text you want to transpose.

② Click 📋.

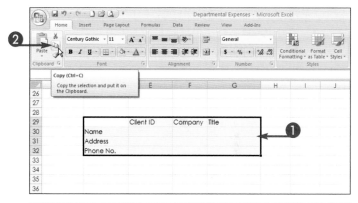

③ Click where you want to insert the transposed text.

Note: The new paste area must be outside the selected cells.

④ Click the **Paste** 🔽.

⑤ Click **Transpose**.

● Excel pastes the text in the reverse order, with column labels becoming row labels and row labels becoming column labels.

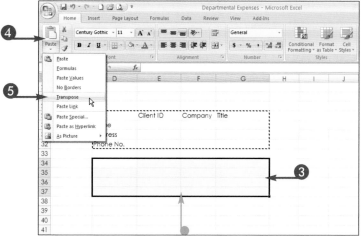

Set Column Width and Row Height

You can change the width of any column or the height of any row in a worksheet. By default, Excel starts all new worksheets with uniform column width and row height. You might need to widen a column to fit a line of text, or you might need to deepen a row to fit a graphic.

Every time you open a new workbook, Excel defines a default column size of 8.43, measured in characters, and a default row height of 15.00, measured in points. You can set your own widths and heights as needed.

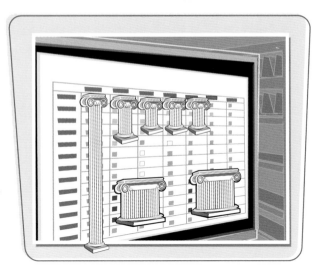

Set Column Width and Row Height

Set a Column Width

1. Click the column you want to edit.

Note: See Chapter 3 to learn how to select columns and rows.

2. Click **Home**.

3. Click **Format**.

4. Click **Column Width**.

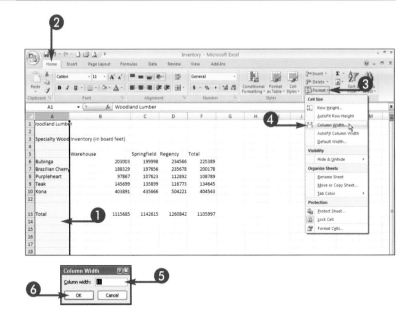

The Column Width dialog box opens.

5. Type a width value for the column.

6. Click **OK**.

Excel assigns the new column width.

Set a Row Height

1 Click the row you want to edit.

Note: See Chapter 3 to learn how to select columns and rows.

2 Click the **Home** tab.

3 Click **Format**.

4 Click **Row Height**.

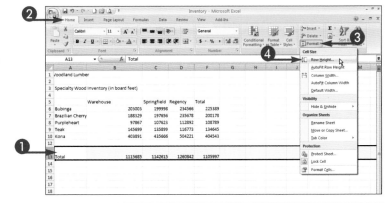

The Row Height dialog box opens.

5 Type a height value for the row.

6 Click **OK**.

Excel assigns the new row height.

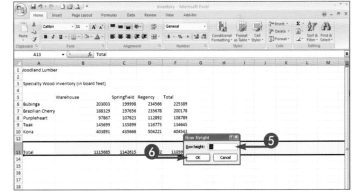

Is there a quicker way to resize a column or row?

For faster column and row resizing, you can drag the borders to the size you want. For example, to resize a column, position the 🖑 over the left or right edge of the column header (🖑 becomes ↔). Then click and drag the border to set a new column width. You can do the same to resize row height.

How do I make a single column or row best fit my text?

Excel offers you a special command to make your column or row automatically resize to the existing text. For example, if you type text into cell A1 that exceeds the width of the column, you can activate the AutoFit Selection command to quickly resize that particular column. Click inside the cell, click on the **Home** tab, click **Format**, and then click **AutoFit**. You can also double-click the right column border or bottom row border to quickly activate the AutoFit command.

Hide Columns and Rows

You can hide columns and rows in your worksheets to keep confidential information out of view. For example, you can hide a column or row to prevent the data from appearing on a printout.

Hide Columns and Rows

Hide a Column

1 Click the column you want to hide.

Note: See Chapter 3 to learn how to select columns and rows.

You can also select multiple columns to hide.

2 Click the **Home** tab.

3 Click **Format**.

4 Click **Hide & Unhide**.

5 Click **Hide Columns**.

● You can also hide an entire sheet in your workbook by clicking **Format**, **Hide & Unhide**, and then **Hide Sheet**.

● Excel hides the column by shifting the other columns over.

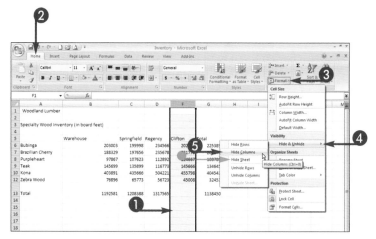

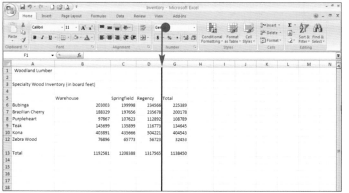

Hide a Row

① Click the row you want to hide.

Note: See Chapter 3 to learn how to select columns and rows.

You can also select multiple rows to hide.

② Click the **Home** tab.

③ Click **Format**.

④ Click **Hide & Unhide**.

⑤ Click **Hide Rows**.

● Excel hides the row by shifting up the other rows.

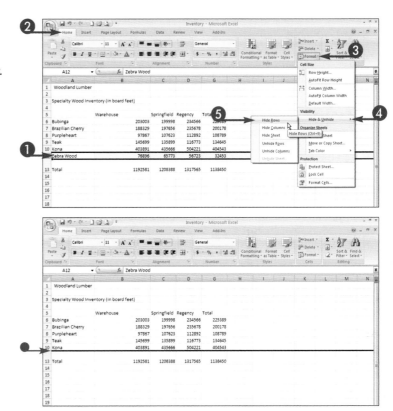

TIP

How do I unhide a column or row?

To display hidden columns and rows again, follow these steps:

① Click the column or row next to the hidden column or row.

② Click **Home**.

③ Click **Format**.

④ Click **Hide & Unhide**.

⑤ Click **Unhide Rows**, or **Unhide Columns**.

Excel displays the full column or row again.

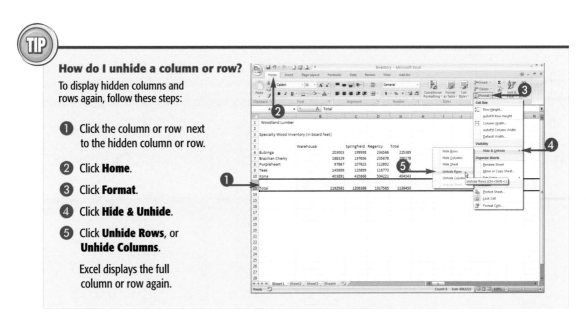

Freeze a Column or Row

You can freeze a column or row to keep the labels in view as you scroll through larger worksheets. The area you freeze is nonscrollable, but the unfrozen areas of the worksheet are still scrollable.

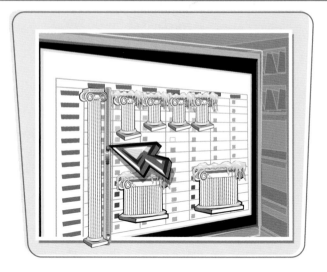

Freeze a Column or Row

① Click to the right of the column or below the row you want to freeze.

② Click the **View** tab.

③ Click **Freeze Panes**.

④ Click **Freeze Panes**.

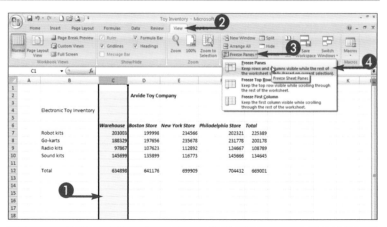

● Excel freezes the area above or to the left of where you applied the Freeze Panes command.

The area below or to the right of the frozen pane is scrollable.

● If you want to freeze only the top row or the first column, use those commands in the Freeze Panes gallery.

● To unlock the columns and rows, click **Freeze Panes** on the View tab, and then click **Unfreeze Panes**.

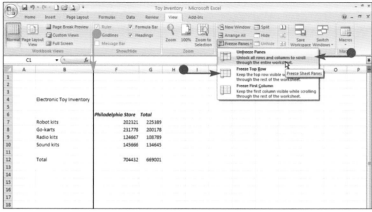

You can view two different areas of a worksheet on-screen at the same time using the Split command. For example, you might want to view both the top and bottom of the worksheet to compare data. When you split panes in Excel, both areas of the split are scrollable.

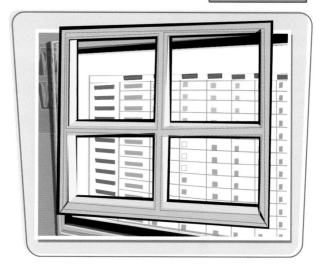

Split a Worksheet into Panes

① Click to the right of the column or below the row you want to split.

② Click the **View** tab.

③ Click **Split**.

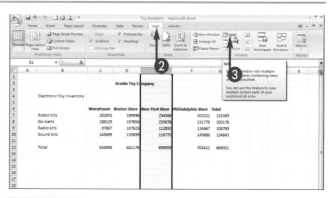

● Excel splits the worksheet into two or more scrollable areas, depending on where you clicked in step **1**.

To remove the split, on the **View** tab click **Split**.

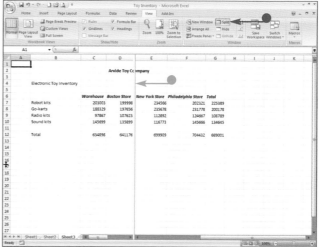

Find and Replace Data

You can use Excel's Find tool to search through your worksheet for a particular number, formula, word, or phrase. You can use the Replace tool to replace instances of text or numbers with other data. For example, you might need to sort through a long worksheet, replacing a reference with another name.

Find Data

1. Click the **Home** tab.

2. Click **Find & Select**.

3. Click **Find**.

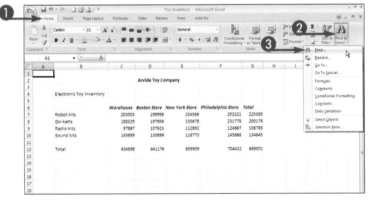

The Find and Replace dialog box opens with the Find tab displayed.

4. Type the data you want to find.

5. Click **Find Next**.

● Excel searches the worksheet and finds the first occurrence of the specified data.

You can click **Find Next** again to search for the next occurrence.

6. When finished, click **Close** to close the dialog box.

Note: *Excel might display a prompt box when the last occurrence is found. Click OK.*

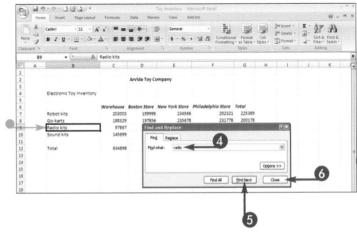

Replace Data

1 Click the **Home** tab.

2 Click **Find & Select**.

3 Click **Replace**.

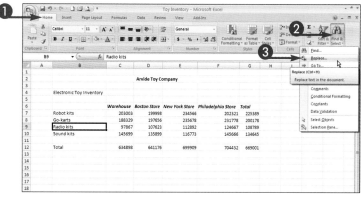

The Find and Replace dialog box opens with the Replace tab displayed.

4 Type the data you want to find, as well as the replacement data.

5 Click **Find Next**.

● Excel locates the first occurrence of the data.

6 Click **Replace** to replace the occurrence.

You can click **Replace All** to replace every occurrence in the worksheet.

7 When finished, click **Close**.

Note: Excel might display a prompt box when the last occurrence is found. Click OK.

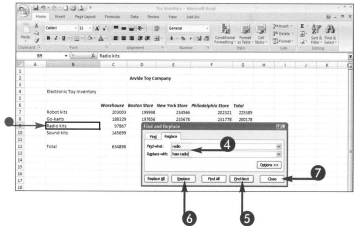

Where can I find detailed search options?

You can click **Options** in the Find and Replace dialog box to reveal additional search options you can apply. For example, you can search according to rows or columns, matching case, and more. You can also search for specific formatting or special characters using the format buttons. To hide the additional search options, click **Options** again.

How can I search for and delete data?

To search for a particular word, number, or phrase using the Find and Replace dialog box and remove the data completely from the worksheet, start by typing the text in the **Find what** text box. Leave the **Replace with** box empty. When you activate the search, Excel looks for the data and replaces it without adding new data to the worksheet.

CHAPTER 7

Formatting Worksheets

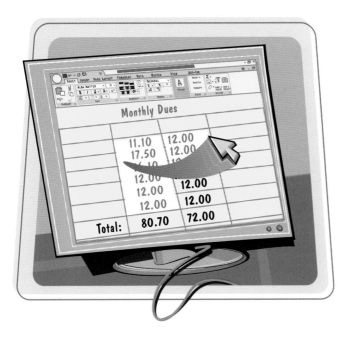

You can make your worksheets more presentable by applying one or several of Excel's many formatting features. This chapter shows you how to improve the appearance of your worksheet data by changing the font and size of the data, adding color and shading, and giving your worksheets a more professional, polished look.

Apply Bold, Italics, and Underlining

One of the quickest and easiest ways to add formatting to your worksheet data is to apply bold, italics, or underlining. For example, you might underline a column heading or bold a title in a worksheet.

You can apply formatting to selected data, cells, ranges, columns, rows, or an entire worksheet.

Apply Bold, Italics, and Underlining

① Select the cell or data you want to format.

Note: See Chapter 3 to learn how to select cells.

② Click the **Home** tab.

③ Click a formatting button:

Click the **Bold** icon (**B**) to bold the data.

Click the **Italic** icon (*I*) to italicize the data.

Click the **Underline** icon (<u>U</u>) to add underlining to the data.

You can also choose combinations of the formatting buttons or apply all three to your data.

Excel immediately applies the formatting to the data.

● In this example, bold formatting is added to the cell.

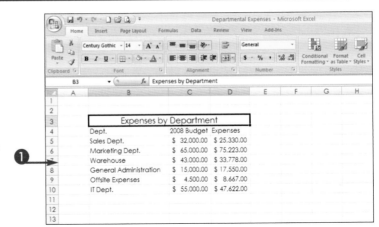

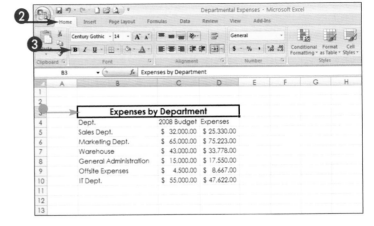

● In this example, bold and italic formatting is added to the cell.

	A	B	C	D	E	F	G	H
1								
2								
3		*Expenses by Department*						
4		Dept.	2008 Budget	Expenses				
5		Sales Dept.	$ 32,000.00	$ 25,330.00				
6		Marketing Dept.	$ 65,000.00	$ 75,223.00				
7		Warehouse	$ 43,000.00	$ 33,778.00				
8		General Administration	$ 15,000.00	$ 17,550.00				
9		Offsite Expenses	$ 4,500.00	$ 8,667.00				
10		IT Dept.	$ 55,000.00	$ 47,622.00				
11								
12								
13								

● In this example, bold, italic, and underline formatting is added to the cell.

	A	B	C	D	E	F	G	H
1								
2								
3		*Expenses by Department*						
4		Dept.	2008 Budget	Expenses				
5		Sales Dept.	$ 32,000.00	$ 25,330.00				
6		Marketing Dept.	$ 65,000.00	$ 75,223.00				
7		Warehouse	$ 43,000.00	$ 33,778.00				
8		General Administration	$ 15,000.00	$ 17,550.00				
9		Offsite Expenses	$ 4,500.00	$ 8,667.00				
10		IT Dept.	$ 55,000.00	$ 47,622.00				
11								
12								
13								

TIPS

How do I remove the formatting from my data?

You can apply the same steps for assigning bold, italics, or underlining to turn the formatting off again. Simply select the data or cell and reactivate the appropriate button. The formatting buttons toggle the command on or off. If you make a mistake with any of the formatting you just applied, you can click the **Undo** icon (⟲).

How can I control the style of the underline?

You can use the Format Cells dialog box to select a line style for any underlining you want to apply. To open the dialog box on the Home tab, click the dialog launcher (▣) in the Font group. You can click the ▼ next to the Underline icon to choose a line style for the underlining effect.

You can control the font and size of your worksheet data. For example, you can make the worksheet title larger than the rest of the data, or you can resize the entire worksheet to a more legible font size, making the data easier to read.

Change the Font and Size

Change the Font

① Select the cell or data you want to format.

Note: *See Chapter 3 to learn how to select cells.*

② Click the **Font** ▾.

● You can use the scroll arrows and scroll bar to scroll through all the available fonts; the Live Preview feature previews the fonts on selected cells.

③ Click a font.

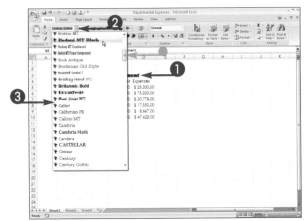

● Excel immediately applies the font.

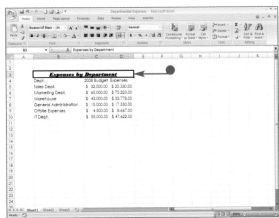

Change the Font Size

1. Select the cell or data you want to format.

Note: *See Chapter 3 to learn how to select cells.*

2. Click the **Font Size** ▾.
3. Click a size.

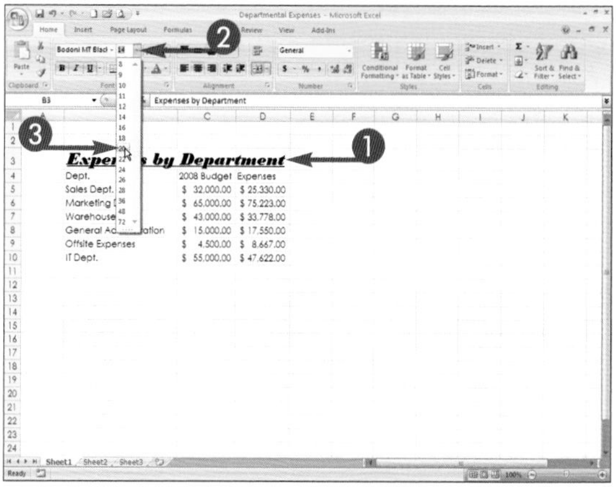

- Excel immediately applies the new size to the selected cell or data.

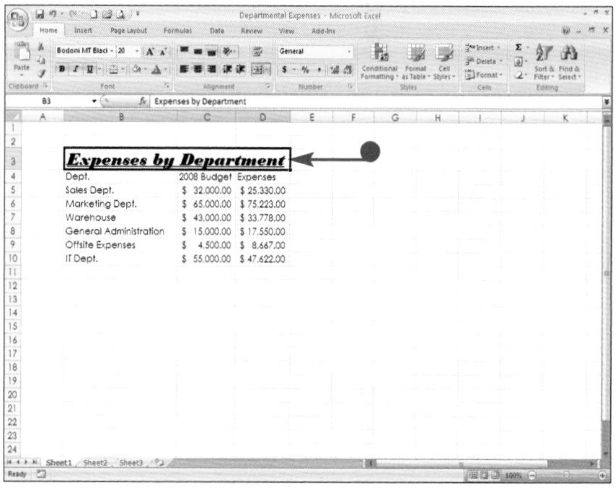

TIP

How do I apply numerous formatting options all at once?

You can use the Format Cells dialog box to apply a new font, size, or any of the basic formatting controls, such as bold, italics, and underlining. Follow these steps to display the dialog box:

1. With the cells you want to format selected, on the Home tab click the Font dialog box launcher (▫) Format.

   The Format Cells dialog box opens.

2. Click the **Font** tab.

- You can use the various options within the Font tab to control the font, size, and style of the data.

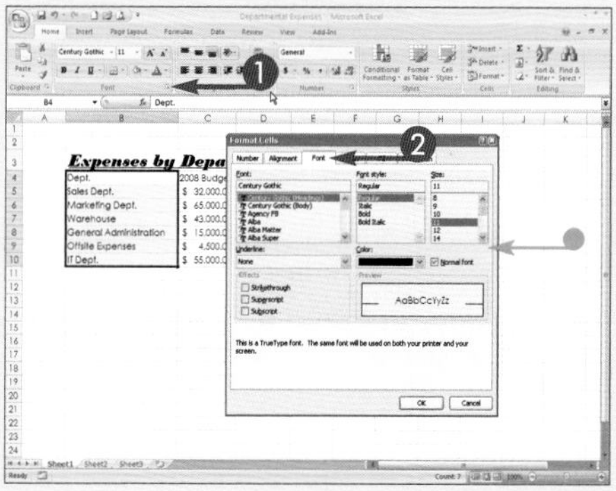

Change Number Formats

You can use number formatting to control the appearance of numerical data in your worksheet. For example, if you have a column of prices, you can apply currency formatting to the data to format the numbers with dollar signs and decimal points. Excel offers 12 different number categories, or styles, to choose from.

Change Number Formats

① Select the cell, range, or data you want to format.

Note: *See Chapter 3 to learn how to select cells. See Chapter 5 to learn about ranges.*

② Click the **Home** tab.

③ Click the **Number Format** ▾.

Note: *You can apply number formatting to single cells, ranges, columns, rows, or an entire worksheet.*

The Number gallery opens.

④ Click a number category.

⑤ If you don't see the category you want on this list, click **More Number Formats**.

The Format Cells dialog box opens.

⑥ Click the **Number** tab.

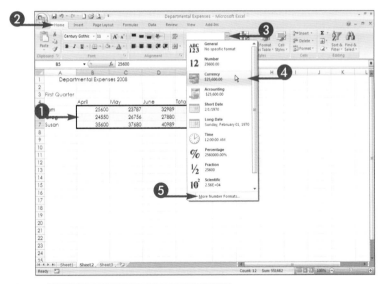

7 Click a number Category.

8 Click **OK**.

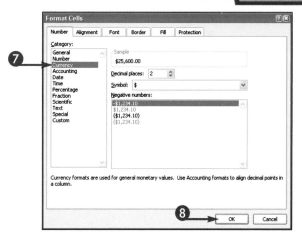

- Excel applies the number formatting to the numerical data in the cell or range.

- To quickly apply dollar signs to your data, click the **Accounting Number Format** icon ().

- To quickly apply percent signs to your data, click the **Percent Style** icon (%).

- To quickly apply commas to your number data, click the **Comma Style** icon.

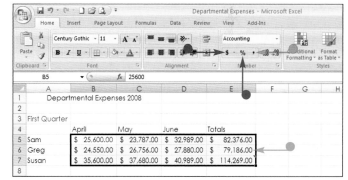

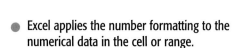 TIP

What sort of number formats can I apply to my numeric data?

Each number format style is designed for a specific use. The table below explains each number category:

Style	Description
General	The default category (no specific formatting is applied)
Number	General number display with two default decimal points
Currency	Adds dollar signs and decimals to display monetary values
Accounting	Lines up currency symbols and decimal points in a column
Date	Use to display date values
Time	Use to display time values
Percentage	Multiplies cell value by 100 and displays percent sign
Fraction	Displays value as a specified fraction
Scientific	Uses scientific or exponential notation
Text	Treats values as text
Special	Works with list and database values
Custom	Enables you to create your own custom format

Increase or Decrease Decimals

You can control the number of decimals that appear with numeric data using the Increase Decimal and Decrease Decimal commands. For example, you might want to increase the number of decimals shown in a cell, or reduce the number of decimals in a formula result.

Increase or Decrease Decimals

① Select the cell or range you want to format.

Note: *See Chapter 3 to learn how to select cells. See Chapter 5 to learn about ranges.*

② Click a decimal button.

Click the **Increase Decimal** icon (⌨) to increase the number of decimals.

Click the **Decrease Decimal** icon (⌨) to decrease the number of decimals.

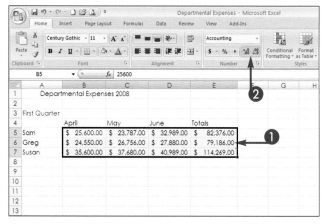

Excel adjusts the number of decimals showing in the cell or cells.

● In this example, only one decimal is removed. To remove another, click ⌨ again.

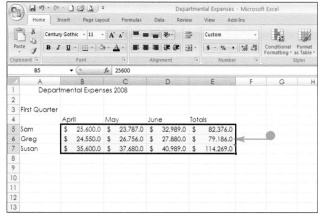

Change Data Color

You can change the color of your data, whether the data is numeric or text. For example, you can select a brighter color for any cell data you want to bring attention to, or select a different color for the column headers in your worksheet.

When adding color to worksheets, always consider the color's effect on the legibility of your data. You want your worksheet to be easy to read, not jarring or distracting to the eye.

Change Data Color

① Select the cell, range, or data you want to format.

Note: See Chapter 3 to learn how to select cells. See Chapter 5 to learn about ranges.

② Click the **Home** tab.

③ Click the **Font Color** ▼.

To apply the current color shown, click the **Font Color** icon (△).

④ Click a color from the palette.

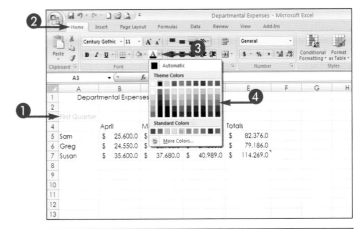

● Excel applies the color to the data.

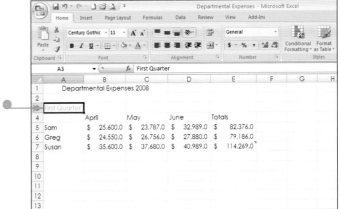

Apply Workbook Themes

You can use Excel's Theme Gallery to apply a combination of formatting settings (colors, fonts, and effects) that give your spreadsheet a professional and cohesive appearance. You can choose from 20 built-in themes or browse themes online. Document themes are used across Office products so all your documents can have a consistent appearance.

Apply a Theme

① Open the workbook you want to format.

Note: See Chapter 2 to learn how to open an existing workbook.

② Click the **Page Layout** tab.

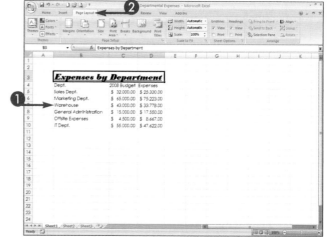

③ Click **Themes**.

The Themes Gallery opens.

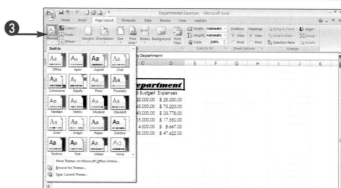

④ Move your mouse cursor over the various themes to see them previewed in your worksheet (this feature is called Live Preview).

⑤ Click the Theme you want to apply.

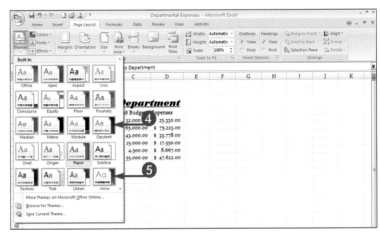

● Excel applies the formatting to the workbook.

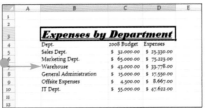

TIP

Can I customize Theme?

Yes. You can modify a theme and save it with a new name so you can select it from the Themes gallery at any time. Follow these steps:

① Apply a theme and make any changes to it you like using the Colors, Fonts, or Effects galleries on the Page Layout tab.

② Click **Themes** on the Page Layout tab, and at the bottom of the Themes Gallery, click **Save Current Theme**.

③ In the Save As dialog box that appears, save the theme with a new name.

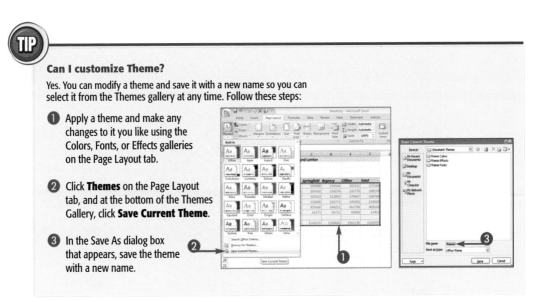

Align Cell Data

You can control the alignment of data within your worksheet cells. By default, Excel automatically aligns text data to the left and number data to the right. Data is also aligned vertically to sit at the bottom of the cell. You can change horizontal and vertical alignments to improve the appearance of your worksheet data.

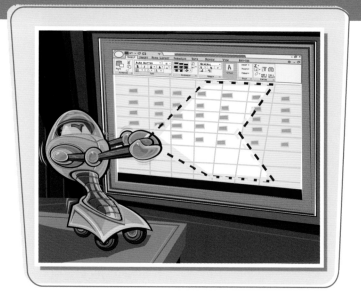

Align Cell Data

Set Horizontal Alignment

1 Select the cells you want to format.

Note: See Chapter 3 to learn how to select cells.

2 Click the **Home** tab.

3 Click an alignment icon in the Alignment group:

Click the **Left Align** icon (▤) to align data to the left.

Click the **Center** icon (▤) to center-align the data.

Click the **Right Align** icon (▤) to align data to the right.

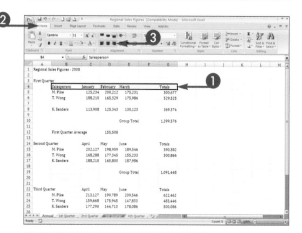

Excel immediately applies the alignment to your cells.

● In this example, the cell data is now centered.

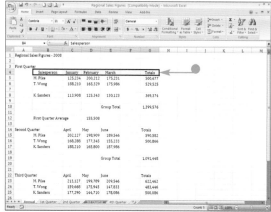

Set Vertical Alignment

① Select the cells you want to format.

Note: See Chapter 3 to learn how to select cells.

② Click the **Home** tab.

③ Click an alignment icon in the Alignment group.

Click the **Top Align** icon () to align data at the top of the cell.

Click the **Middle Align** icon (▤) to center-align the data.

Click the **Bottom Align** icon (▤) to align data at the bottom of the cell.

Excel immediately applies the alignment to your cells.

● In this example, the cell data is now top aligned.

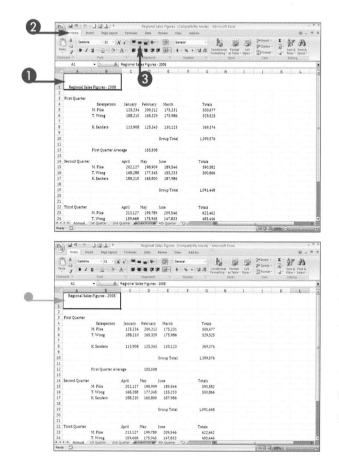

TIPS

How do I set indents for my cell text?

You can use the Increase Indent and Decrease Indent commands to add indents to lines of text in your worksheet. To indent text, click the **Home** tab and then click the **Increase Indent** icon (▤) on the Formatting toolbar. To decrease an indent, click the **Decrease Indent** icon (▤).

Can I justify my text to line up with both the left and right margins in a cell?

Yes. To justify cell text, you must open the Format Cells dialog box and click the **Alignment** tab, as outlined in the steps in this section. You can then click the **Horizontal** ▼ and click **Justify** to assign justification to your cell text.

Rotate Cell Data

You can rotate cell data to flip text sideways or print it from top to bottom instead of from left to right. For example, you might want to rotate long column headers to keep your column widths shorter.

Rotate Cell Data

1 Select the cells you want to rotate.

Note: See Chapter 3 to learn how to select cells.

2 Click the **Home** tab.

3 Click the **Alignment** dialog box launcher (⊡).

The Format Cells dialog box opens.

4 Click the **Alignment** tab.

5 Click the orientation you want to apply or type the degrees of rotation you want to set.

● To orient data to display from top to bottom instead of from left to right, click this box.

6 Click **OK**.

Excel applies the orientation alignment to the cells.

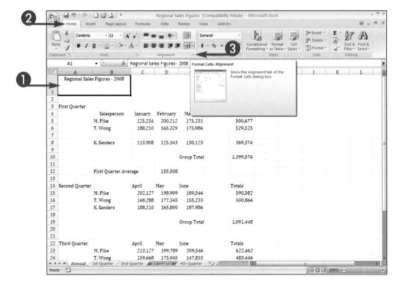

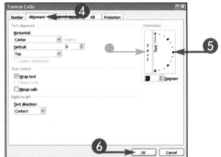

By default, any text you type into a cell stays on one line. For longer text entries, this means the text might appear to span several columns. To make the text stay in one cell and wrap to fit the cell width, you can activate the text-wrapping feature using the Format Cells dialog box.

Control Text Wrap

① Select the cells you want to format.

Note: See Chapter 3 to learn how to select cells.

② Click the **Home** tab.

③ Click the **Alignment** dialog box launcher.

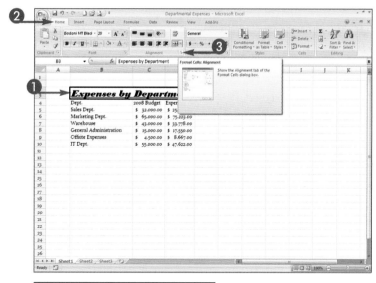

The Format Cells dialog box opens.

④ Click the **Alignment** tab.

⑤ Click the **Wrap text** option (☐ changes to ☑).

⑥ Click **OK**.

Excel applies text wrapping to the cell or cells.

Add Borders

You can add borders to your worksheet cells to help define the contents or more clearly separate the data from surrounding cells. By default, Excel displays a grid format to help you enter data, but the borders defining the grid do not print.

You can add borders to emphasize cells. You can add borders to all four sides of a cell, or choose to add borders to just one or two sides. Any borders you add to the sheet print out along with the worksheet data.

Add Quick Borders

① Select the cells you want to format.

Note: See Chapter 3 to learn how to select cells.

② Click the **Home** tab.

③ Click the **Borders** ▾.

To apply the current border selection shown, click the **Borders** icon (▦).

④ Click a border style.

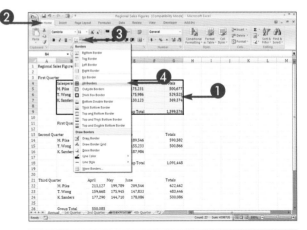

● Excel immediately assigns the borders to the cell.

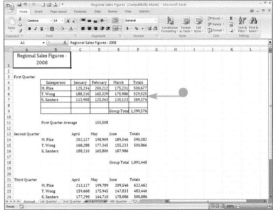

Create Custom Borders

① Select the cells you want to format.

Note: *See Chapter 3 to learn how to select cells.*

② Click the **Home** tab.

③ Click the **Font** dialog box launcher.

The Format Cells dialog box opens.

④ Click the **Border** tab.

⑤ Click the type of border you want to assign.

You can click multiple border buttons to create a custom border.

● To set a particular line style to the border, click a style here.

● You can also click a preset style to assign.

⑥ Click **OK**.

Excel assigns the border.

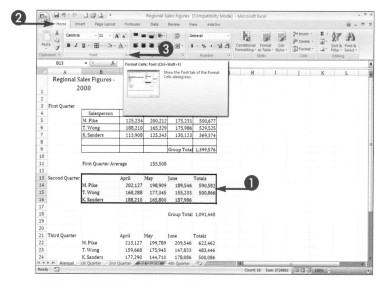

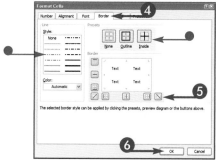

 TIPS

Can I turn the worksheet gridlines on or off?

Yes. By default, Excel displays gridlines to help you differentiate between cells as you build your worksheets. You can turn gridlines off to view how your data will look when printed. Click the **Page Layout** tab, and then in the Sheet Options group, click **View** to deselect the **Gridlines** option (☑ changes to ☐) to turn gridlines off. Excel does not print gridlines unless you specify. To learn more about printing options, see Chapter 9.

Can I change the color of a border?

Yes. In the Format Cells dialog box on the Borders tab, click the **Color** ▼ to display a color palette. Choose from Theme Colors to use a color that fits in with the overall theme, choose a standard color, or click more colors to select from a wider range of standard colors or create a custom color. Click **OK** to save the new border color for the selected cells.

Add Background Color to Cells

You can add a background color to a cell to help draw attention to the cell data. You can add a solid color or a pattern. Excel offers a variety of preset colors and patterns you can choose from to create just the right look for your worksheet data.

Use caution when assigning colors and patterns as backgrounds. Make sure the color or pattern does not make the cell data illegible.

Add Background Color to Cells

Add Quick Color

① Select the cell or range you want to format.

Note: See Chapter 3 to learn how to select cells.

② Click the **Home** tab.

③ Click the **Fill Color** ▾.

● To apply the current fill color shown, click the **Fill Color** icon (⬛).

④ Click a color.

As you move your mouse cursor over the colors in the palette, you can see a preview of the color in the cell.

● Excel immediately assigns the background color to the cell or range.

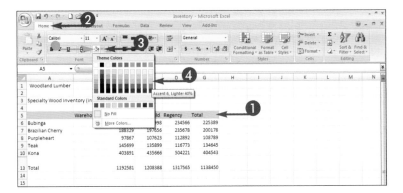

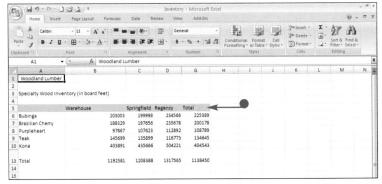

Create Custom Color or Pattern

1 Select the cells you want to format.

Note: See Chapter 3 to learn how to select cells.

2 Click the **Home** tab.

3 Click the **Font** dialog box launcher (▣).

The Format Cells dialog box opens.

4 Click the **Fill** tab.

5 Click the **Pattern Color** ▾.

● To assign a pattern cell shading color, click a color.

The sample area displays a preview of the color.

6 Click the **Pattern Style** ▾.

To assign a pattern style, click a style.

The sample area displays a preview of the pattern style.

7 Click **OK**.

Excel assigns the formatting.

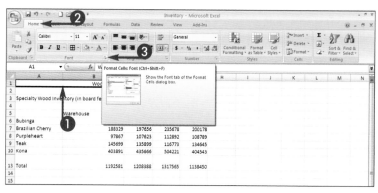

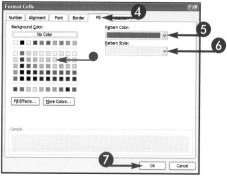

TIPS

Do I have to have a color printer to use background colors and patterns?

No. You can take advantage of the various shades of gray to add background colors to your worksheet cells. You can also experiment with the palette of solid colors to create varying degrees of background shading in grayscale tones.

How do I restore a cell to its default state?

To remove all of the formatting in a cell, including background colors or patterns, first select the cell, next click the **Home** tab, and then click **Cell Styles**. In the gallery of styles that appears click **Normal**. This removes all the formatting that has been applied.

Assign a Background to a Worksheet

You can add a photo background to a worksheet for added interest. For example, if your worksheet documents sales, you might add a picture of a product.

Be sure to select a background that does not detract from the legibility of your worksheet data. You might need to change the color of your worksheet data to keep it from conflicting with the background image. See the section "Change Data Color" to learn more.

Assign a Background to a Worksheet

① Click the **Page Layout** tab.

② Click **Background**.

The Sheet Background dialog box opens.

● You can use the **Look in** ▾ to navigate to the folder or drive where the image is stored.

③ Select the image you want to use as a background.

④ Click **Insert**.

Excel applies the image to the worksheet background.

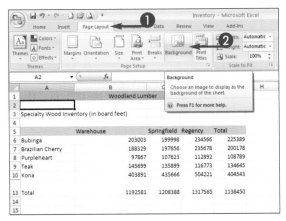

Copy Cell Formatting

You can use the Format Painter feature to copy formatting to other cells in your worksheet. For example, perhaps you have applied a variety of formatting to a range of cells to create a certain look.

When you want to re-create the same look elsewhere in the worksheet, you do not have to repeat the same steps you applied to assign the original formatting. Instead, you can paint the formatting to the other cells with a single procedure.

Copy Cell Formatting

① Select the cell or range containing the formatting you want to copy.

Note: *See Chapter 3 to learn how to select cells.*

② Click the **Home** tab.

③ Click **Format Painter** (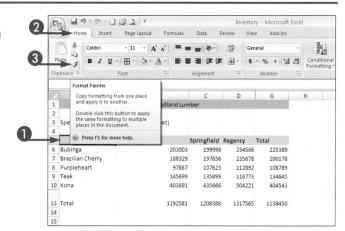).

To copy the same formatting multiple times, double-click .

Excel surrounds the cell or range with a blinking border.

④ Click and drag over the cells to which you want to copy the formatting.

Excel immediately copies the formatting to the new cells.

You can press Esc to cancel the Format Painter at any time.

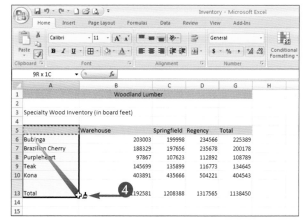

Apply a Style

You can use a style to quickly assign formatting throughout a workbook. A style is a collection of formatting, whether you define a font and size or a background color.

Apply a Style

① Select the cell or cells to which you want to apply a style.

Note: See Chapter 3 to learn how to select cells.

② Click the **Home** tab.

③ Click **Cell Styles**.

The Style gallery opens.

④ Click a style to apply it.

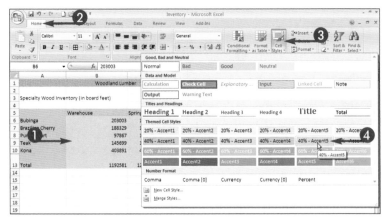

Customize a Style

① Select the cell or cells to which you want to apply a style.

Note: See Chapter 3 to learn how to select cells.

② Click the **Home** tab.

③ Click **Cell Styles**.

The Style gallery opens.

④ Right-click a style.

⑤ Choose **Modify**.

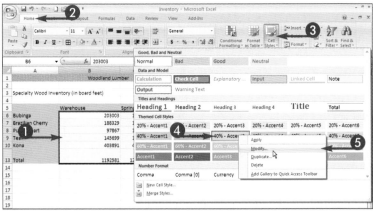

The Style dialog box appears

6 Type a name for the style.

7 Click **Format**.

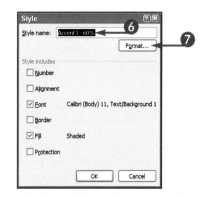

The Format Cells dialog box opens.

8 Apply all the formatting you want to set for the style.

You can use any of the tabs to set formatting options for the style.

9 Click **OK**.

10 Click the modified style in the gallery.

Excel applies the style.

Note: To apply the style to other cells, simply open the Cell Styles gallery and select the style to apply it.

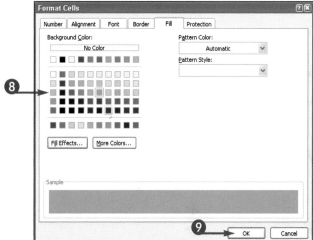

TIPS

How do I remove a style I no longer want?

To remove a style, first open the Cell Styles gallery as shown in the steps in this section. Next, right-click the name of the style you want to delete and choose **Delete** from the menu that appears to remove the style.

Can I apply a table style?

Yes. You can select cells and then, on the Home tab, click **Format as a Table**. From the gallery of table styles that appears, click a style to apply it. Cells formatted as a table allow you to use table tools, such as sorting and filters, from a drop-down menu embedded in the column headings.

Assign Conditional Formatting

You can use Excel's conditional formatting feature to assign certain formatting only when the value of the cell meets the specified condition.

For example, perhaps your worksheet tracks weekly sales and compares them to last year's sales during the same week. You can set up conditional formatting to alert you if a sales figure falls below last year's level, and make the cell data appear in red or bold.

Assign Conditional Formatting

① Select the cell or range to which you want to apply conditional formatting.

Note: See Chapter 3 to learn how to select cells.

② Click the **Home** tab.

③ Click **Conditional Formatting**.

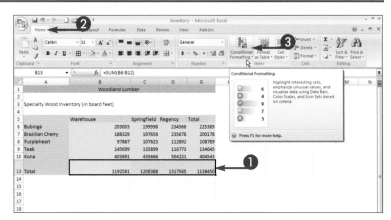

④ Click **Highlight Cells Rules**.

Note that there are other rules you can apply from this menu, depending on what conditions you wish to highlight.

⑤ Specify the operator you want to assign for condition 1.

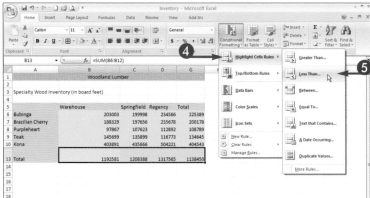

The associated dialog box, such as Less Than, opens.

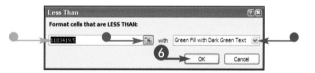

● If you need to select a cell or range, click here to minimize the dialog box and view more of the worksheet.

● Enter a value or text for the condition here.

● Click ☑ and choose a format to apply.

If you want to apply other formatting, click **Custom Format** in this list and choose any settings you wish from the Format Cells dialog box that appears.

⑥ Click **OK**.

● If the cell value changes to meet the condition, Excel applies the conditional formatting.

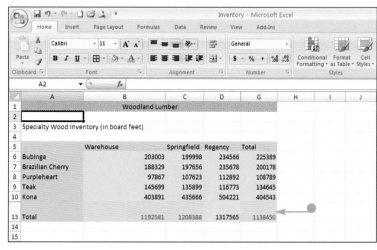

TIPS

What sorts of formatting should I apply for conditional formatting?

For many users, color coding the data is sufficient to draw attention to a cell that meets a condition. You can also format the cell in italics or bold. If your worksheet is exceptionally long, you might also consider applying a background color to the cell to help you highlight the cell when it meets a condition.

How do I remove conditional formatting from a cell?

To remove conditional formatting, first select the cell, next click the **Home** tab, and then click **Conditional Formatting**. Choose **Clear Rules**, and then click **Selected Cells** from the side menu that appears. The conditional formatting is removed.

Enhancing Worksheets with Graphics

You can use graphics in Excel to illustrate your data and add visual impact to your worksheets. This chapter shows you how to add existing artwork as well as create your own artwork using Excel's drawing tools.

Insert Image Files

You can illustrate your Excel worksheets with images stored on your computer. For example, if you have a photo or graphic file from another program that relates to your Excel data, you can insert it into the worksheet.

Image or picture files, also called *objects* in Excel, come in a variety of file formats, such as GIF, JPEG or JPG, and PNG. After you insert an image, you can resize and reposition it as well as perform other types of edits on the image.

Insert Image Files

① Click the cell in the worksheet where you want to add an image.

You can also move the image to a particular location after inserting it onto the worksheet.

② Click the **Insert** tab.

③ Click **Picture**.

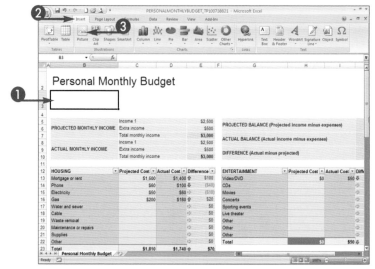

The Insert Picture dialog box opens.

④ Navigate to the folder or drive containing the image file you want to use.

● To browse for a particular file type, click here and choose a file format.

⑤ Click the image file you want to insert.

⑥ Click **Insert**.

● Excel adds the image to the worksheet and adds the Picture Tools Format tab to the Ribbon.

You might need to resize or reposition the image to fit with your data, or resize the cell in which you want the image to appear.

Note: See the section "Move and Resize Objects" to learn more about manipulating images.

To remove an image you no longer want, click the image and press Delete.

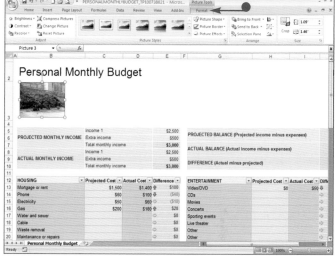

TIP

Can I insert other objects into my worksheets?

Yes. In addition to picture files, you can insert other types of objects, such as Word tables, scanned images, digital photographs, or another Excel worksheet. Follow these steps to insert an object:

❶ Click **Insert**.

❷ Click **Object**.

The Object dialog box opens.

❸ Click the **Create from File** tab.

❹ Type the path to the object you want to insert, or use the Browse button to navigate to the file.

❺ Click **OK**.

Excel inserts the object into your worksheet.

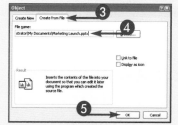

You can add interest to your worksheets by inserting clip art images. Clip art is predrawn artwork that Excel installs with the Office clip art collection. In addition, you can look for more clip art on the Web using the Clip Art task pane.

Insert Clip Art

① Click the cell in which you want to add clip art.

You can also move the clip art to a particular location after inserting it onto the worksheet.

② Click the **Insert** tab.

③ Click **Clip Art**.

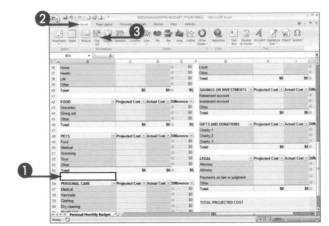

The Clip Art task pane opens.

④ To search for a particular category of clip art, type a keyword or phrase here.

● To search in a particular collection, click here and click a collection.

● You can also search for clip art on the Office Web site by clicking this link.

⑤ Click **Go**.

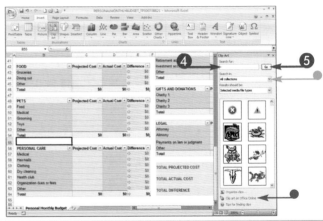

The Clip Art task pane displays any matches for the keyword or phrase you typed.

● Click and drag the scroll bar to move through the list of matches.

● To view information about a clip art image, position 🔓 over the image.

⑥ To add a clip art image to your worksheet, click the image.

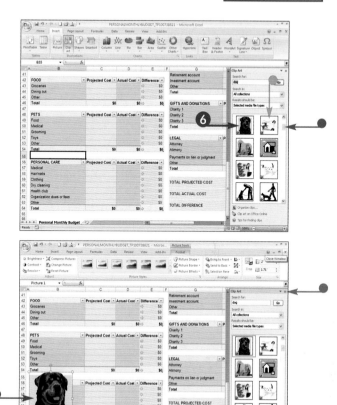

● Excel inserts the clip art and displays a Picture Format tab on the Ribbon.

You can resize or move the clip art, if needed, or resize a cell to fit the clip art.

Note: *See the section "Move and Resize Objects" to learn more.*

To deselect the clip art, click another area on the worksheet.

● You can click the Clip Art task pane's **Close** button (☒) to close it.

How do I search for a particular type of clip art, such as a photo or sound file?

To search for a particular type of media, click the **Results should be** ▾. The drop-down menu displays a list of different media types. You can select or deselect which types to include in your search results. If you leave the **All media types** option selected (☑), Excel searches for a match among all the available media formats.

How do I find details about the clip art?

To find out more about the clip art's properties in the Clip Art task pane, position the 🔓 over the image, click the drop-down arrow, and then click **Preview/ Properties**. This opens the Preview/Properties dialog box, and you can learn more about the file size, filename, file type, file creation date, and more.

View Clip Art with the Clip Organizer

You can use the Microsoft Clip Organizer to view clip art collections on your computer. You can also insert clip art from the Organizer window and place it in your worksheet.

View Clip Art with the Clip Organizer

① Display the Clip Art task pane.

Note: See the section "Insert Clip Art" to display the Clip Art task pane.

② Click **Organize clips**.

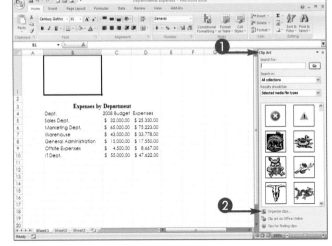

The Microsoft Clip Organizer window opens.

③ Click **Collection List** if the list is not already displayed.

④ Click ⊞ to expand the collection list.

● Some categories include subcategories, in which case you can click a category ⊞ to expand the list.

● The Clip Organizer displays thumbnails of available clip art.

- displays the images as thumbnails.

- displays the images as a text list.

- displays the images as a text list, along with details such as format and file size.

  To view information about a clip art image, position the ⊳ over the image.

- To add a clip art image to Excel, drag and drop the clip art onto your worksheet.

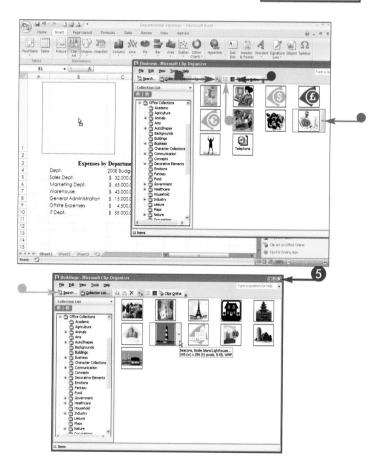

- You can click **Search** to display settings for conducting a search for clip art on your computer.

⑤ When finished viewing clip art, click the **Close** button (✕).

  The Microsoft Clip Organizer window closes.

TIPS

Is there a way to add the same clip art image every time I use Excel?

Yes. You can create a macro that inserts the clip art image — or any other image file, such as a logo — when you activate the macro keystrokes. To learn how to create a macro, see Chapter 15.

Can I copy clip art from one collection to another?

Yes. You can copy clip art from one collection and paste it into another collection using the Microsoft Clip Organizer. Simply click the clip art you want to copy and then click the **Copy** and **Paste** buttons on the Microsoft Clip Organizer's toolbar to copy and paste the clip art.

Download Clip Art from the Web

You can look for additional clip art to use in your workbooks by perusing the Microsoft Office Web site. You can download clip art and import it into a clip art collection in the Microsoft Clip Organizer.

You must log on to your Internet connection to view the Office Web pages and download clip art.

Download Clip Art from the Web

1 Display the Clip Art task pane.

Note: See the section "Insert Clip Art" to learn how to display the Clip Art task pane.

2 Click **Clip art on Office Online**.

Note: You must first log on to your Internet connection before clicking the Web site link.

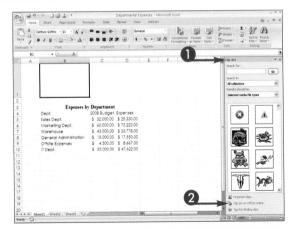

Your default Web browser opens to the Office Online Web site.

3 Click a clip art category link.

● To look for a particular media format, click the **Search** button (▼) and choose a format.

You can search through the clip art to find a particular image to download, using the navigation links to move through the clip art pages.

④ Click a check box (☐ changes to ☑) to select an image for downloading.

The clip art is added to your download basket.

⑤ When you are ready to download the images, click **Download** and follow the download instructions as prompted.

● When the download is complete, the clip art is added to the Clip Organizer window, where you can view it in the Downloaded Clips category.

Note: See the section "View Clip Art with the Clip Organizer" to learn how to add clip art from the Clip Organizer to your Excel worksheets.

Where else can I find clip art collections to use with Excel?

You can purchase clip art collections from computer and office supply stores, as well as find clip art collections to buy on the Internet. For example, if you need to use a lot of work-related clip art, you can look for a business collection of clip art, and you can also find collections geared toward certain industries, such as architecture and banking. You can also find clip art for free on the Web, but most sites require registration or a subscription for their services.

Can I use any artwork I find on the Internet in my workbooks?

No. Be careful about using copyrighted images. Most images on the Internet are protected by copyrights, and you cannot reuse them without permission. If you do use a copyright-protected image, be sure to get permission and then cite its source.

Draw Shapes

You can use Excel's drawing tools to draw your own shapes and graphics for your worksheets. You can choose from a library of predrawn shapes in the Shapes palette.

The Drawing Tools Format tab also includes tools for controlling the color and thickness of the lines and shapes you draw.

Draw Shapes

① Click the **Insert** tab.

② Click the **Shapes** button (▼).

The Shapes gallery appears.

Note: See Chapter 1 to learn more about Excel galleries.

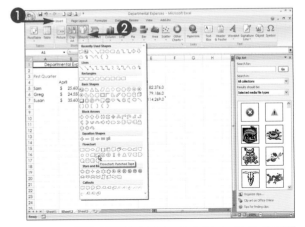

③ Click on a shape in any category.

The ⍺ becomes +.

④ Click and drag diagonally on the worksheet to draw the desired shape.

Holding down the Shift key as you drag retains the original shape proportions.

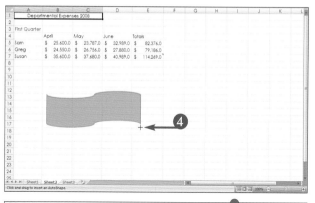

● When you release the mouse, Excel completes the shape.

● A Drawing Tools Format tab appears on the Ribbon.

Note: *To move and resize the object, or edit it with the tools on the Drawing Tools Format tab, see the section "Move and Resize Objects."*

● You can click these buttons to define the line thickness and color of the shape after drawing the shape.

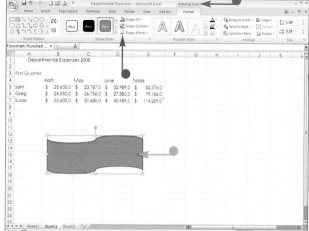

TIP

How do I change a shape to a different shape once it is drawn?

The Insert Shapes group on the Drawing Tools Format tab includes an Edit Shape button. Follow these steps to change from one shape to anther using this tool:

① Click **Drawing Tools Format**.

② Click **Edit Shapes** (▦) and choose Change Shape.

③ Click any shape from the gallery of shapes that appears.

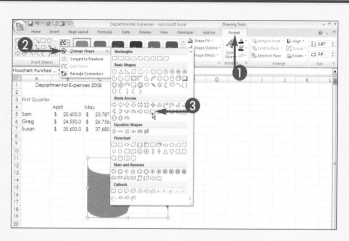

Add a WordArt Object

You can use the WordArt feature to turn text into interesting graphic objects to use in your worksheets. For example, you can create arched text to appear above a range of data. You can create text graphics that bend and twist or that display subtle shadings of color.

① Click the **Insert** tab.

② Click **WordArt**.

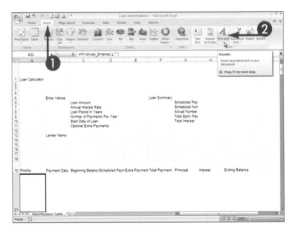

The WordArt gallery opens.

③ Click a WordArt style.

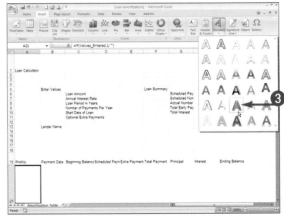

A rectangular WordArt placeholder appears containing the words "Your Text Here."

④ Type your WordArt text.

⑤ Click the **Drawing Tools Format** tab to modify the WordArt text.

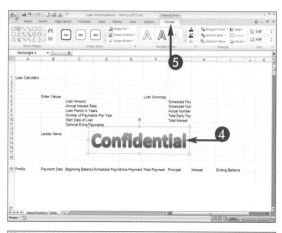

⑥ Use tools in the Shape Styles group to modify the WordArt object:

● Click **Shape Effects** and apply effects such as shadow, rotation, and bevel.

● Click **Shape Outline** to modify the outline of the text.

● Click **Shape Fill** to change the color of the inside of the letters or apply a gradient or pattern.

You can resize or move the image, if needed.

Note: See the section "Move and Resize Objects" to move and resize objects.

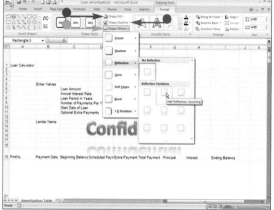

 TIPS

How do I change the height and width of my WordArt text?

On the Drawing Tools Format tab, use the Height and Width tools in the Size group to change the size of the WordArt font. Select the WordArt object first and then click the up or down arrows on the Height (⬚) and Width (⬚) tools to modify the font size.

How to I change the WordArt style?

You can click the **Quick Styles** icon in the WordArt group on the Drawing Tools Format tab to quickly access the drop-down gallery and select another style to apply. You can also click any of the Shape Styles previews to apply a different background color to the shape.

Move and Resize Objects

You can move and resize any clip art, image, or shape — called *objects* in Excel — you place on an Excel worksheet. When you select an object, it is surrounded by handles that you can, in turn, use to resize the object.

Move and Resize Objects

Move an Object

1 Click the edge of the object you want to move.

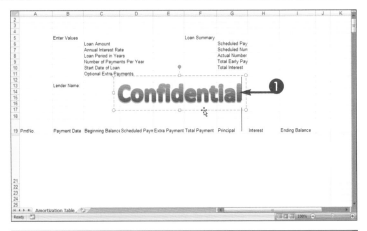

● The ⌖ becomes ✛.

2 Drag the object to a new location on the worksheet.

Excel moves the object.

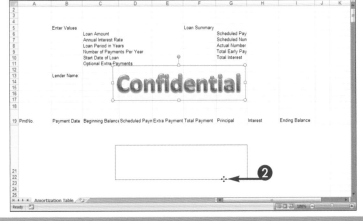

Resize an Object

① Click the object you want to resize.

② Position the ⌖ over a selection handle.

The ⌖ becomes ⇳ .

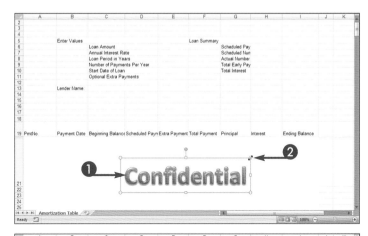

③ Drag the handle to resize the object.

Excel resizes the object.

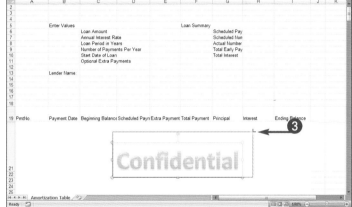

Can I also use the Cut, Copy, and Paste commands to move or copy an object?

Yes. You can easily cut, copy, and paste objects around your worksheets or workbooks. Simply select an object and apply the commands. You can click the **Cut** (✂), the **Copy** (📋), or the **Paste** (📋) button on the Home tab of the Ribbon, or you can use keystroke shortcuts such as pressing Ctrl + X to cut and Ctrl + V to paste.

Can I resize an object and keep the scaling proportional?

To maintain an object's height-to-width ratio when resizing, press and hold Shift while dragging a resizing corner handle. To resize from the center of the object in two dimensions at once, press and hold Ctrl while dragging a corner handle.

Rotate and Flip Objects

You can rotate and flip objects to change your worksheet's appearance. For example, you might flip a clip art image to face another direction, or rotate an arrow object to point elsewhere on the page.

Rotate and Flip Objects

Rotate an Object

1 Click the object you want to rotate.

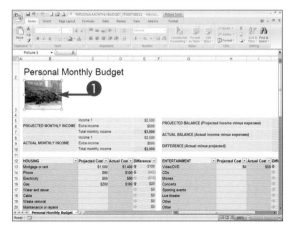

A rotation handle appears on the selected object.

2 Click and drag the handle to rotate the object.

Note: *To constrain the rotation to 15-degree angles, press and hold* Shift *while rotating the object.*

Excel rotates the object.

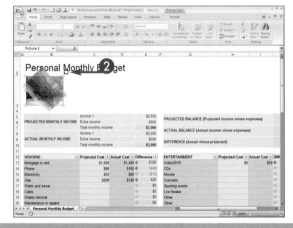

Flip an Object

1 Click the object you want to flip.

2 Click the **Picture Tools Format** tab.

3 Click **Rotate**.

4 Click **Flip Vertical** or **Flip Horizontal**.

Excel previews the effect on the picture.

You can also rotate an object 90 degrees left or right.

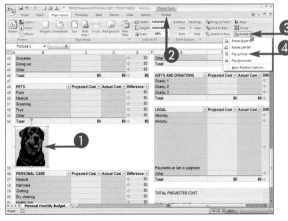

● Excel flips the object.

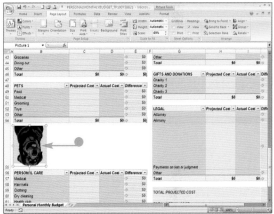

TIPS

How do I rotate text in Excel?

You can rotate text in a cell, or you can create a WordArt object to rotate. Learn more about rotating cell text in Chapter 7. Learn how to create a WordArt object in the section "Insert a WordArt Object." After you create the WordArt, you can rotate it using the steps shown in this section.

Is there a way to prevent anyone from moving or rotating an object on my worksheet?

After you position an object just the way you want it on the worksheet, other users who have access to your file can make changes to the data, including changes to the objects in your worksheets. The only way to prevent someone from making changes to your worksheet is to assign a password or apply the read-only option.

To learn more about protecting Excel worksheets with passwords, see Chapter 4.

Crop a Picture

You can crop a picture you add to an Excel worksheet to create a better fit or to focus on an important area of the image. The Crop tool, located on the Picture toolbar, can help you crop out parts of the image you do not need. You can also crop clip art images.

Crop a Picture

1 Click the image you want to edit.

2 Click the **Picture Tools Format** tab.

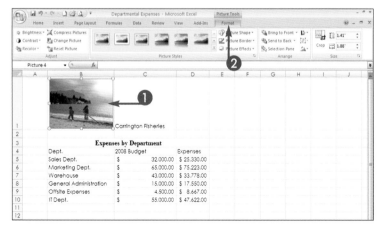

3 Click the **Crop** icon ( ).

Excel surrounds the image with crop handles.

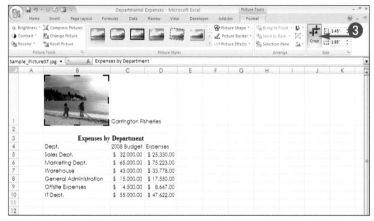

④ Click and drag a crop handle inward to crop out an area of the image.

⑤ Release the mouse button.

Excel crops the image.

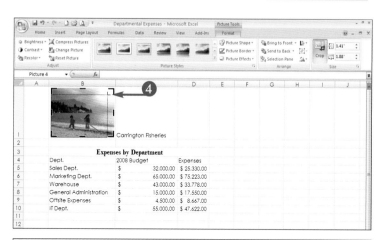

⑥ Continue cropping other edges of the image, as needed.

You can click ⊞ again to turn off the Crop tool.

Note: *See the section "Move and Resize Objects" to learn how to move or resize an image.*

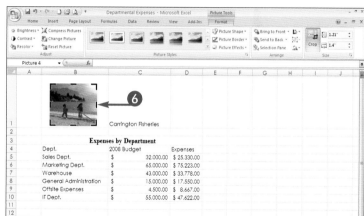

 TIPS

How can I reduce the overall file size of an image I use in a worksheet?

Image files are notorious for consuming large amounts of file space, and inserting a large image into a worksheet adds to the size of the Excel file. You can apply the Compress Pictures tool on the Picture Tools Format tab to reduce the resolution of an image or discard the extra information that is generated when you crop an image. The Compress Pictures dialog box offers several options for helping to control the overall file size of an image.

How can I return the image to its original state before cropping?

You can also click the **Undo** icon (↰) on the Quick Access toolbar to undo each edit you made to the image immediately after you make it, or press Ctrl + Z, an Undo keystroke shortcut.

Add Shadow and 3-D Effects

You can add shadow and 3-D effects to your Shapes, lines, arrows, and any other shapes you draw with the drawing tools. Adding shadow and 3-D effects can give an object the illusion of depth on the worksheet page.

Add Shadow and 3-D Effects

Add a Shadow

① Select the object to which you want to add shadow effects.

The Drawing Tools Format tab appears on the Ribbon.

② Click the **Shape Effects** button.

③ Click **Shadow**.

④ Click a shadow style.

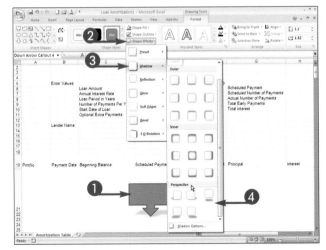

● Excel applies the shadow to the object.

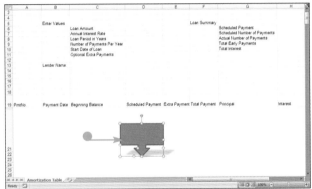

Add a 3-D Effect

1. Select the object to which you want to add shadow 3-D effects.

   The Drawing Tools Format tab appears on the Ribbon.

2. Click **Shape Effects**.

3. Click **Preset** or **3-D Rotation**.

4. Click a 3-D style.

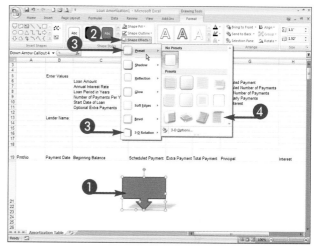

● Excel applies the 3-D style to the object.

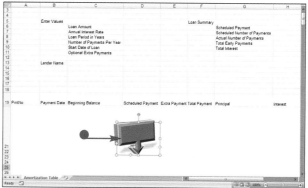

TIPS

Is there a way to fine-tune a shadow effect?

When you click the **Shape Effects** button and click **Shadow**, you can click **Shadow Options** to display a Format Shape dialog box that allows you to choose a Shadow preset and adjust options, such as the transparency, blur, and angle of the shadow.

Can I edit the way in which my 3-D effect is applied to a shape?

Just like the shadow effect, you can fine-tune the 3-D effect using the Format Shape dialog box. You first click **Shape Effects**, then **Preset**, then **More 3-D Settings** to display this. The dialog box includes tools for changing the depth of the effect, the contours, and the color.

Format an Object

You can edit the objects you add to a worksheet by accessing the Format dialog box. For example, for a Shape, you can make adjustments to the shape's color, alignment, and line thickness. Depending on the object, the Format Shape dialog box might display different formatting options you can apply.

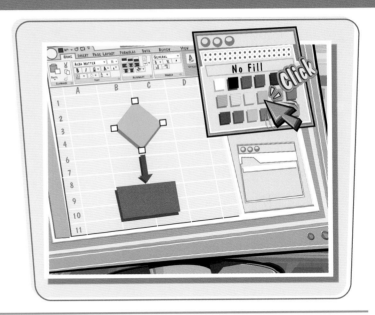

Format an Object

1 Right-click the object and then click **Format Shape**.

You can also click the corresponding Effects button – for example, the Picture Effects or Shape Effects buttons – on the Drawing Tools Format tab, choose a category, and then choose the **More** command at the bottom of the menu to display the Format Shape dialog box.

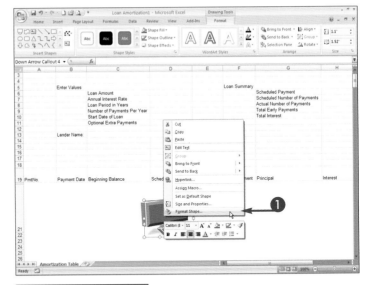

● The Format Shape dialog box opens.

A category such as Fill allows you to fill the object with color, patterns, or gradients effects.

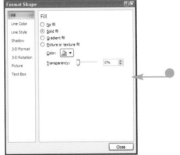

② Click another category on the left.

You can use the Line Style category, shown in this figure, to make changes to the line or Shadow to change shadow effects, for example.

③ Click **Close**.

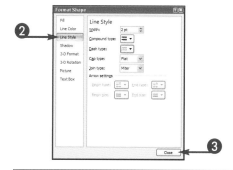

● Excel applies any new settings to the object.

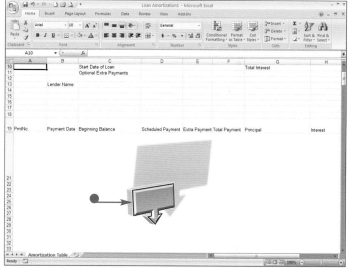

TIPS

What can I do with picture styles to format my graphic objects?

Styles is a gallery of preset formatting you can quickly apply to any object. The Styles are named according to the type of object, such as Shape Styles and Picture Styles. They are located on the Drawing Tools Format tab or Picture Tools Format tab, and the corresponding tab will appear depending on which type of object you select. Just move your cursor over a style to see it previewed in your object.

What kind of formatting changes can I make to clip art objects?

You can make most of the changes to predrawn art that you can make to other drawings or pictures by adding a border around the clip art. You can use the Lines and Shadow options in the Format Shape dialog box to add a border, or you can use the 3-D tools to shift the perspective on the object. Depending on the clip art background, you can also make changes to the artwork's fill color or transparency setting.

Group and Ungroup Objects

If you add multiple objects to a worksheet, such as multiple shapes you draw with Excel's drawing tools, you can turn them into a single group. Grouping objects allows you to move the objects as a unit rather than as separate pieces. You might also group objects to perform edits all at once.

Group and Ungroup Objects

① Click the first object you want to include in a group.

● Handles surround the selected object.

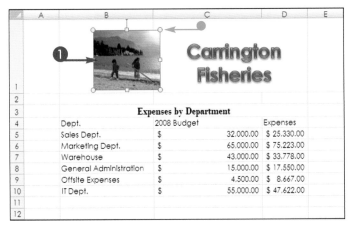

② Press and hold **Shift** and click the next object you want to include in the group.

● Another set of handles surrounds the selected object.

You can repeat step **2** to select any additional objects you want to group.

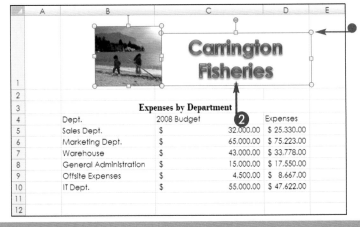

③ Click the **Drawing Tools Format** tab.

④ Click **Group**.

⑤ Click **Group**.

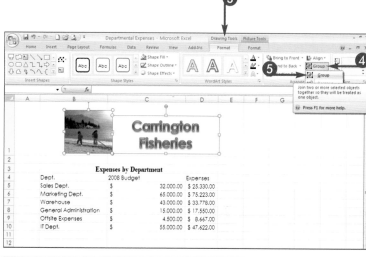

Excel groups the objects as one unit.

● Excel replaces the multiple selection handles with a single set of handles around the entire group.

You can now move, resize, and edit the group of objects.

Note: To ungroup a group, on the Drawing Tools Format tab click **Group** and then click **Ungroup**.

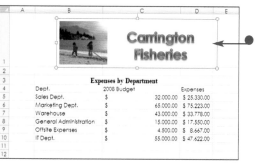

 TIPS

How can I reposition multiple objects on my worksheet?

You can layer objects to change the appearance of the objects. For example, you might want to stack several drawn shapes and layer them so that one shape appears on top of all the others. You can click **Bring to Front** on the Drawing Tools Format tab to bring a selected object to the front of the stack, or **Send to Back** to send it to the back of the stack.

Is there another way to select and group multiple objects?

Yes. If you have several objects scattered in a worksheet, click the **Home** tab, click **Find & Select**, and then click **Select Objects**. Drag a selection handle around the objects to temporarily create a group, which you can resize or move as a unit. When you click outside the group, the objects become separate again.

CHAPTER 9

Previewing and Printing

As you finalize your worksheet for printing, you can use a variety of Excel tools and options to improve your worksheet's appearance on a printed page. For example, you can preview a worksheet, add headers and footers, control page breaks, insert comments, and more. This chapter shows you a few ways you can check and enhance a worksheet before committing it to paper.

You can insert page breaks to control what data appears on each page in a worksheet. By default, Excel breaks pages based on margins, column widths, and the amount of data that fits within the page parameters. You can insert two types of page breaks: vertical or horizontal. Vertical page breaks divide the page at a particular column heading. Horizontal page breaks divide the page at a specific row.

Insert Page Breaks

Insert a Page Break

① Click the column heading to the right of where you want to break the page vertically, or click the row label above where you want to break the page horizontally.

② Click the **Page Layout** tab.

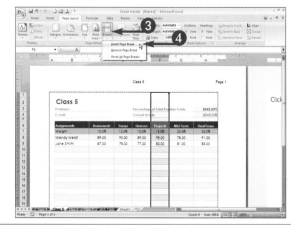

③ Click **Breaks** (⊞).

④ Click **Insert Page Break**.

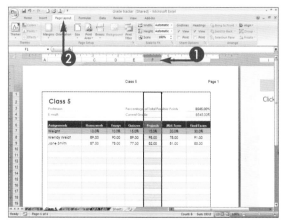

● Excel adds a page break, which appears as a dotted vertical or horizontal line on the worksheet.

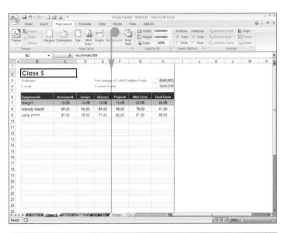

View Page Breaks

❶ Click **Page Break Preview** ().

Excel switches to Page Break Preview mode and displays a Welcome prompt box.

❷ Click **OK**.

● Default page breaks appear as blue dotted lines on the worksheet.

● Manual page breaks appear as solid blue lines.

To move a page break, click and drag the line to a new location on the page.

● To return to normal worksheet view, click **Normal View** ().

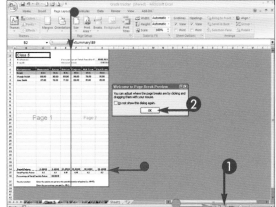

TIPS

How do I remove a page break?

The following technique only works on manual page breaks. You cannot delete default page breaks Excel inserts automatically. To move a manual page break on a worksheet, click the Page Break Preview button (📖) to display that view. Next, follow this procedure:

❶ Click a row below or column to the right of the page break you want to delete.

❷ Click the **Page Layout** tab.

❸ Click Breaks (▦).

❹ Click **Remove Page Break**.

Excel removes the manual break.

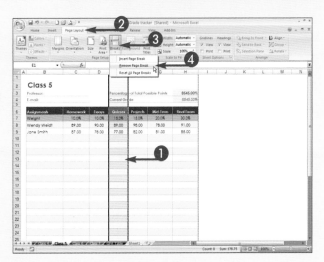

Preview a Worksheet

You can use Print Preview mode to preview worksheets before printing them. In Print Preview, you can see how your worksheet will look when it is printed, including any headers, footers, and margins you have set. You can also move margins to make adjustments to the page.

Preview a Worksheet

① Click the **Office** button (⬚).

② Click ▾ on **Print** (🖶).

③ Click **Print Preview**.

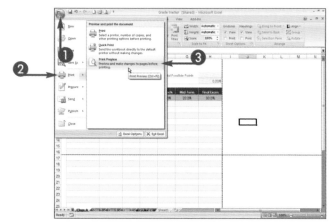

Excel opens the worksheet in Print Preview mode.

● You can click the preview page to change the magnification of your view.

● You can click **Next Page** and **Previous Page** to view another page in your worksheet.

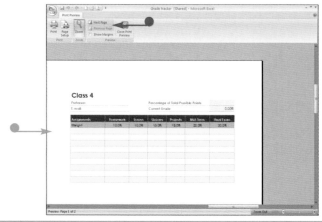

● You can click **Show Margins** (☐ changes to ☑) to hide or display margins on the page.

● Margins appear as dotted lines on the page.

● You can click a line and drag with the changed mouse cursor (⬍) to adjust the page margin.

Note: See the section "Insert Page Breaks" to learn how to view page breaks in Excel.

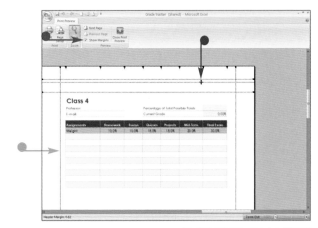

● You can click **Page Setup** to access Page Setup options.

● You can click **Print** to print the file.

④ Click **Close Print Preview**.

Print Preview closes.

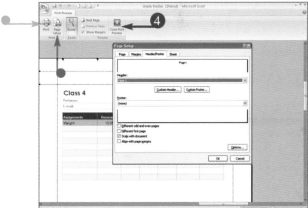

What is Page Break Preview?
Page Break Preview is a view mode you can use to view and make adjustments to page breaks on your worksheets. You can also use the view to see the actual print area of your worksheet and define the area for printing. To learn more about Page Break Preview, see the section "Insert Page Breaks." To learn how to specify a range of cells to print out, see the section "Define a Print Area."

Can I set a specific zoom level in Print Preview?
No. **Zoom** (🔍) in Print Preview mode only toggles between two views of the worksheet. To see your worksheet cells in a closer view, you must return to Normal view mode and click **Zoom In** (⊕) or **Zoom Out** (⊖) next to the view buttons at the bottom of the screen to change magnification levels in a worksheet.

Set Up Printing Options

You can use the Page Layout Ribbon to control any printing options you want to assign to a worksheet. For example, you can set margins, change the page orientation, and control how various elements of your worksheet print, such as grid lines and headings.

To learn how to add headers and footers to your worksheet using the Insert Ribbon, see the section "Add Headers and Footers."

Set Up Printing Options

① Click the **Page Layout** tab.

*Note: You can also access the page setup options through the Print Preview window; simply click **Page Setup** ( ). See the previous section to learn more about Print Preview.*

② Click the **Page Setup** dialog box launcher ( ).

The Page Setup dialog box appears.

③ Click the **Page** tab.

● To control the page orientation, click one of these options (⃝ changes to ⦿).

● To change the paper size, click here and select a size.

● To change the print quality, click here and select a quality setting.

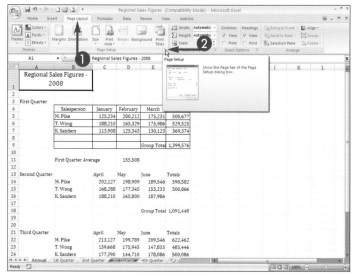

④ Click the **Margins** tab.

● You can make changes to the margins by typing an exact measurement or by clicking the arrows.

● You can also select these options (☐ changes to ☑) to center the data vertically or horizontally on the page.

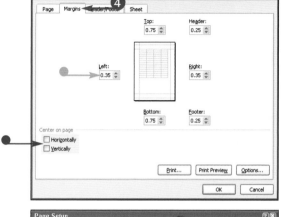

⑤ Click the **Sheet** tab.

● To print the gridlines with your worksheet, activate this option (☐ changes to ☑).

● You can control the order in which the worksheets print by selecting one of these options (○ changes to ◉).

● To print headings with your worksheet, choose this option (☐ changes to ☑).

⑥ Click **OK**.

Note: See the section "Print a Worksheet" to learn how to print a file.

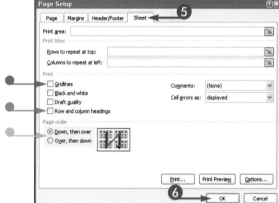

Which page orientation is best to use with Excel worksheets?

The page orientation you select depends on how you want to display the data on a page. For regular 8½-x-11-inch paper, landscape orientation prints the page at 11 x 8½ inches, and portrait orientation prints 8½ x 11 inches. Select landscape orientation when you need to print several columns across the page. Select portrait orientation to print more rows down a page.

Can I tell Excel to fit all the worksheet data onto a printed page?

Yes. You can use the scaling options in the Page tab of the Page Setup dialog box to set up your data to fit all on one page. You can accomplish this by shrinking or expanding the printed data image. After adjusting settings in the scaling options, you can click **Print Preview** to preview what the printed worksheet will look like.

Print a Worksheet

If you have a printer connected to your computer, you can print your Excel worksheets. You can send a file directly to the printer using the default printer settings, or you can open the Print dialog box and make changes to the printer settings.

① Click 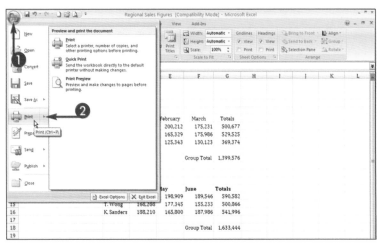.

② Click .

To print a file without adjusting any printer settings, click **Quick Print** () on the Quick Access toolbar.

The Print dialog box opens.

● You can select a printer from this list.

● You can specify a print range and what part of the workbook to print using these options (○ changes to ◉).

● You can specify a number of copies to print or find more printer-specific options by clicking **Properties**.

③ Click **OK**.

Excel sends the file to the printer for printing.

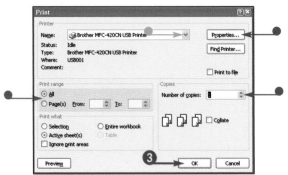

Define a Print Area

You can define a print area to print only a certain portion of a worksheet. For example, you might want to print only a range of cells. You can define the print area to prevent Excel from printing the entire worksheet.

Define a Print Area

1. Select the cells you want to include in the print area.

Note: See Chapter 4 to learn how to select cells and ranges.

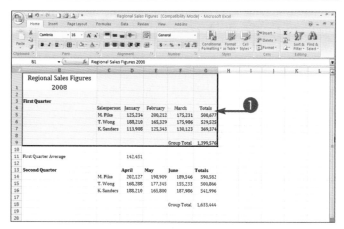

2. Click the **Page Layout** tab.

3. Click **Print Area**.

4. Click **Set Print Area**.

Excel saves the print area.

The next time you print, Excel prints only the defined cells.

Note: To clear a defined area, click  on the Page Layout tab and then click **Clear Print Area**.

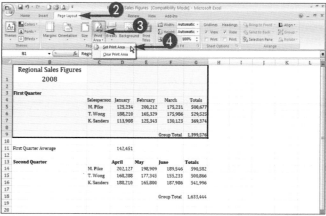

Communicating Information with Charts

You can use charts to turn your worksheet data into a striking visual representation for others to view. Whether you are depicting rising or falling sales, or actual costs compared to projected costs, charts make it easy for others to interpret and understand your data. This chapter shows you how to create and format charts to their best advantage.

Understanding Excel Charts

You can use charts to turn your spreadsheet data into instant, persuasive visual presentations. You can create dozens of different charts in Excel, from pie charts to bar charts and more. If you are new to using charts to visualize data, this section gives you an overview of how charts work in Excel.

Data Series

The foundation of any chart is the worksheet data you use to create the chart. Called a *data series*, chart data is the content of a group of related cells, such as one row or column of data in your worksheet. For example, to make a pie chart of monthly household expenses, your worksheet data needs to consist of columns and rows tracking expenses such as electricity, gas, water, mortgage, groceries, and so on. You decide which cells to include in the chart, and Excel's chart tools can help you build a pie chart using the cell's contents and labels.

Customize Charts

You can customize any chart you create in Excel. You can make changes to the formatting of the chart text, change the chart type, replot the data, and much more. You can angle text, change text color, or adjust the colors and patterns of the bars and lines displayed in a chart. You can also add new chart elements, such as callouts, labels, and titles. Layout and Style galleries feature new to Excel 2007 offers easy-to-apply, predesigned formatting.

Chart Types

Excel offers 11 different types of charts, and each type includes a variety of styles. You can use the following table to help choose the best chart for the type of data you want to present.

Chart Type	Description
Column	Compares data in two or more categories, or shows changes over time.
Bar	Similar to column charts. Displays the data horizontally instead of vertically.
Line	Similar to column charts, but instead of bars, the data series appears as dots on lines. Good for showing changes across time.
Pie	Perfect for showing percentages of a whole. You can select several pie chart styles, including 3-D.
Scatter	Shows correlations between two value sets, one on the y-axis and the other on the x-axis.
Area	Shows changes over time but emphasizes the individual contribution of each data part.
Doughnut	Compares multiple data series.
Radar	Depicts separate axes for each data category radiating out from the center, like a spider web.
Surface	Shows how three sets of data interact. Ideal for showing patterns in data.
Bubble	Similar to scatter charts, bubble charts use three columns of data. Each data point indicates a third dimension.
Stock	Ideal for tracking stock market activity.

Chart Objects

Charts are composed of a variety of elements, also called *objects*. When you edit a chart, you can edit different elements to give you greater control of the visual representation.

Part	Description
Legend	Tells what each data series in your chart represents.
Chart title	Gives a headline to your chart.
Plot area	The background of your chart.
Value axis	The axis listing values for the data series.
Value axis title	A headline identifying the value axis.
Category axis	The axis listing categories for the data series.
Category axis title	A headline identifying the category axis.
Data series	The data you are plotting on a chart.

Create a Chart with Galleries

You can use the chart galleries to quickly assemble and create all kinds of charts in Excel. The galleries offer you a wide variety of charts. You can select the chart category and then the specific type you need for your data.

Create a Chart with Galleries

① Select the range of data you want to chart.

Include any headings and labels, but do not include subtotals or totals.

② Click the **Insert** tab.

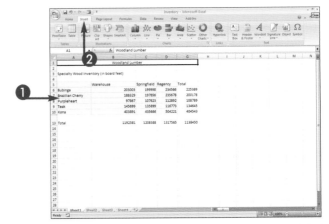

③ Click an item in the Charts group.

The associated gallery opens.

For additional chart types, click the Charts dialog box launcher (⬛).

④ Click a chart sub-type.

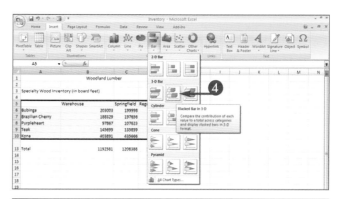

● The chart appears on your worksheet.

● Contextual tools (Design, Layout, and Format tabs) appear in the Ribbon.

● If you want to move the chart to its own sheet, click **Move Chart** on the Design tab and choose **New Sheet**.

Note: To learn how to add titles to your chart, see the section "Change the Axes Titles," later in this chapter.

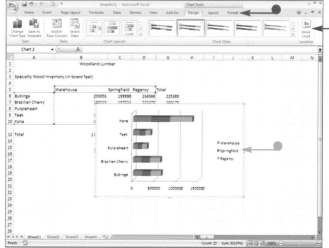

Can I select noncontiguous data to include in a chart?

Yes. The data you select for a chart do not have to be adjacent to each other. To select noncontiguous cells and ranges, select the first range and then press and hold Ctrl while selecting additional ranges to include.

Can I create a default chart style that applies whenever I insert a chart?

Yes. In the Create Charts dialog box, you can click **Set as Default Chart**. Thereafter, when you open the Create Charts dialog box, that chart sub-type is selected by default.

Move and Resize Charts

You can move and resize an embedded chart on your worksheet. For example, you might want to reposition the chart at the bottom of the worksheet or resize it to make the chart easier to read.

You cannot move or resize charts you create on their own sheets.

Move a Chart

① Click an empty area of the chart.

● Excel selects the chart and surrounds it with handles.

② Position the mouse over the edge of the chart, and it becomes a cursor with four arrows ✛ .

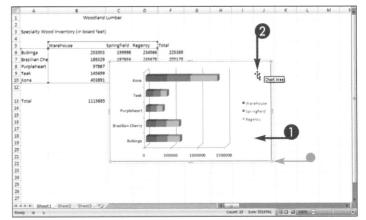

③ Click and drag the chart to a new location on the worksheet.

Excel moves the chart.

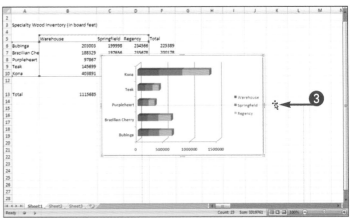

Resize a Chart

1 Click an empty area of the chart.

● Excel selects the chart and surrounds it with handles.

2 Click and drag a handle to resize the chart.

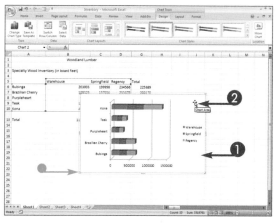

Excel resizes the chart.

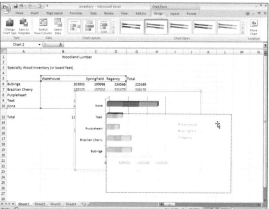

TIPS

How do I move a chart to a different worksheet?

Select the chart, and the Design tab appears. Click **Move Chart**, and in the Move Chart dialog box that appears, either enter a chart name for a new sheet, or click **Object In** (○ changes to ◉) and pick a sheet from the drop-down list to move the chart to. Click **OK** to move the chart.

How can I proportionately resize a chart?

You can press and hold [Shift] while dragging any of the corner selection handles of a selected chart to resize the chart proportionately. Dragging outwardly makes the chart proportionately bigger, and dragging inwardly makes the chart proportionately smaller.

You can change the chart type at any time to present your data in a different way. For example, you might want to change a bar chart to a line chart.

Change the Chart Type

1. Click an empty area of the chart to select the chart.

2. Click the **Design** tab.

3. Click **Change Chart Type**.

   The Change Chart Type dialog box appears.

4. Click a new chart type.

5. Click **OK**.

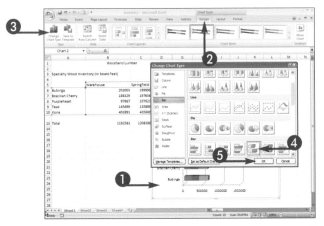

● Excel applies the type to the existing chart.

Note: *You can also right-click a chart and click* **Change Chart Type** *to access this dialog box.*

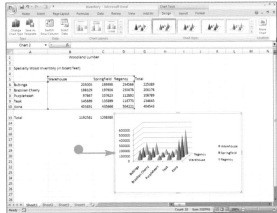

You can change the titles of the x- or y-axis on your chart. For example, you might prefer to give the axes more descriptive titles, or if your titles are too long, you might want to shorten the title text. You can change chart title information using the Edit Data Source dialog box.

Change the Axes Titles

① Select the chart you want to edit.

② Click the **Layout** tab.

③ Click **Axis Titles**.

④ Click **Primary Vertical Axis Title** or **Primary Horizontal Axis Title**.

⑤ Select an axis type (for example, Vertical Title or Rotated Title).

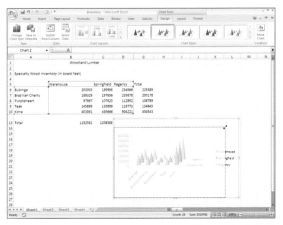

The title placeholder appears.

⑥ Click and drag in the placeholder to select the placeholder text and enter new text.

⑦ Press **Enter** or click outside the placeholder to save the new title.

Excel applies the new titles to the chart.

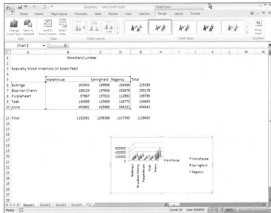

Manipulate 3-D Charts

Certain chart styles use a 3-D effect to give a feeling of depth and perspective to their elements. If you have inserted a 3-D chart style, you have several tools at your disposal that you can use to fine-tune the 3-D elements. For example, you can rotate the elements to different angles or change the position of the items from the ground of the chart.

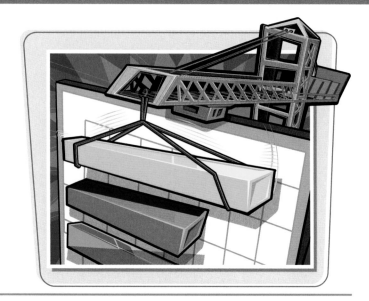

Manipulate 3-D Charts

① Select the chart.

② Click the **Layout** tab.

③ Click **3-D Rotation**.

The Format Chart Area dialog box appears.

④ Click the **3-D Rotation** tab.

⑤ Make any of the following settings:

● Click settings to adjust the rotation of the x- or y-axis (this adjusts the angle at which you view chart elements).

● Click settings to modify the perspective, which is somewhat like zooming in and out of the chart.

● If you have text inside a shape, click the **Keep Text Flat** checkbox (☐ changes to ☑) to keep the text from changing along with a 3-D shape.

● Click to move elements closer or farther away from the chart base.

● Click to increase or decrease the depth of the chart depth.

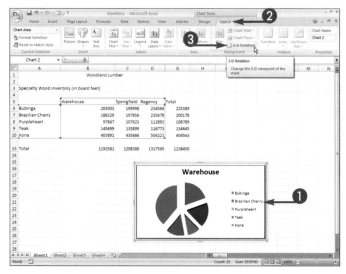

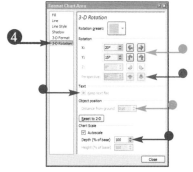

6 Click the **3-D Format** tab.

7 Make any of the following settings:

● Click to choose a bevel style for the top or bottom of the chart border.

● Click to change the depth of the bevel.

● Click to add contours to bevel edges.

● Click to modify the surface texture and lighting effect applied to objects in the chart.

8 Click **Close**.

● Excel applies the new formats.

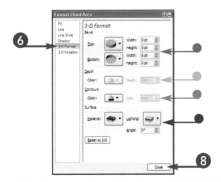

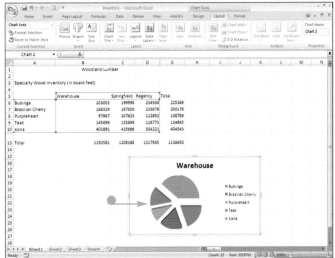

If I do not like the 3-D look, how do I easily get rid of the 3-D appearance?

You can click **Reset** on the 3-D Rotation tab of the Format Chart Area dialog box. This quickly removes all 3-D effects from the chart.

Why are 3-D tools not available for line charts?

Certain types of charts, such as line and scatter charts, do not lend themselves to 3-D effects because the lines that form them are one-dimensional. If you crave 3-D, and one of the other chart types is appropriate to communicating your data, choose another chart type and try again.

Format Chart Objects

You can change the formatting for any of the elements, called *objects* in Excel, contained within a chart. For example, you can change the background color or pattern for the plot area or change the color of a data series on the chart.

① Select the chart.

The Chart Tool tabs become available.

② Click the **Format** tab.

③ Click to select the chart object you want to edit.

④ Click **Format Selection**.

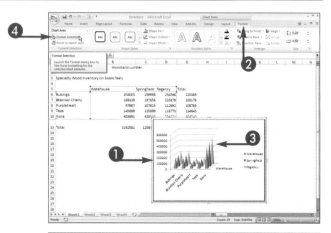

A Format dialog box appears. Depending on the chart object you want to edit, the options offered will vary.

Note: For more about chart objects, see the section "Understanding Excel Charts."

⑤ Make any changes to the chart object, as needed.

● In this example, a new fill color is applied.

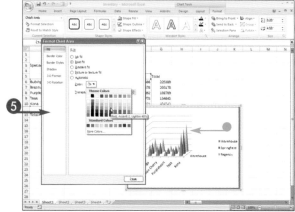

Depending on the chart object you edit, the dialog box offers different options.

● In this example, a new object shape is applied.

⑥ When finished with your edits, click **Close**.

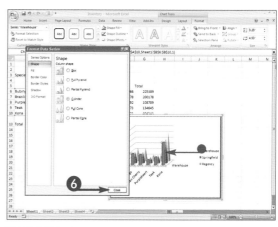

Excel applies any changes to the chart.

● In this example, a new fill color is added to one bar series, and the bar shape has been changed.

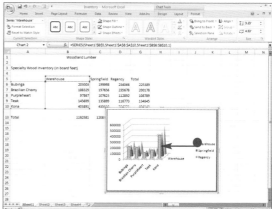

TIPS

How do I change the font for my chart text?

You can click on any text object in a chart, and it opens for editing. Click the **Home** tab and use the Font group of tools to format the text.

How do I print my chart?

To print only the chart, first select the chart on the worksheet and then click 🖺 and **Print**. The Print dialog box opens. Make sure the Selected Chart option is selected (○ changes to ◉) is selected, and then click **OK** to print the chart. If the chart is on its own sheet, you can just click the **Quick Print** icon (▼) to print the sheet. To learn more about printing in Excel, see Chapter 9.

Add Chart Objects

You can add additional objects to your charts, such as data labels, gridlines, or a legend. The Layout tab is where you access tools for adding and working with chart objects.

Add Chart Objects

① Select the chart you want to edit.

② Click the **Layout** tab.

③ Click an item in the Labels or Axes group of tools.

④ Click the object you want to add.

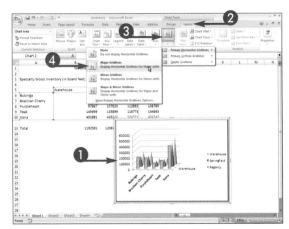

A drop-down menu offers options to display objects. In this example, both major and minor vertical gridlines are selected to be displayed.

● Excel adds the object.

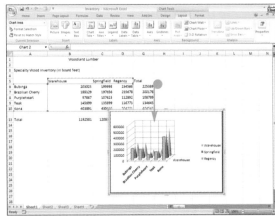

Whenever you make changes to the data referenced in your chart, the chart data is automatically updated. For example, if you change a value, the chart updates to reflect the new value. If you need to add more data to the chart, you can easily update the source cells.

Change the Chart Data

① Select the chart you want to edit.

● Excel surrounds the chart with selection handles and marks the source data in the worksheet with a colored border.

② Click and drag the corner handle of the source range to add or subtract cells.

Note: *If you have moved the chart, you might need to click and drag it to another part of the worksheet to access the source data.*

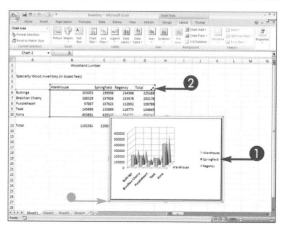

● Excel updates the chart with any changes.

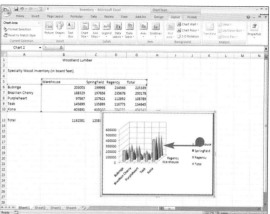

Format Charts with Layouts and Styles

In Excel 2007, new features offer you instant formatting of chart elements. Quick Layouts use sets of formatting for gridlines, labels, and settings, such as perspectives to quickly give your chart a new look. Styles apply preset color schemes and backgrounds to add instant design appeal.

Format Charts with Layouts and Styles

① Select the chart.

② Click the **Design** tab.

③ Click the Chart Layouts ▼ to scroll through chart layouts.

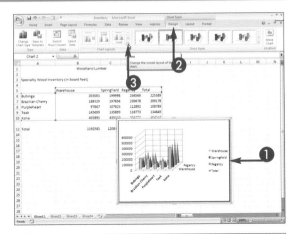

④ Click a layout to apply it.

⑤ Click to display all styles.

⑥ Click a style to apply it.

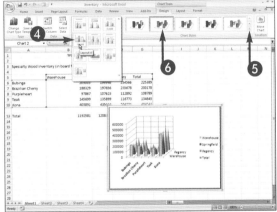

You can add a SmartArt graphic to track the hierarchy of an organization or method or a workflow process, list, or cycle. When you insert a SmartArt graphic, Excel starts you with a few shapes to which you can add your own text. You can add additional shapes and branches to the object as needed.

Insert SmartArt Charts

① Click the **Insert** tab.

② Click **SmartArt**.

③ Click a type of chart.

④ Click a sub-type of chart.

⑤ Click **OK**.

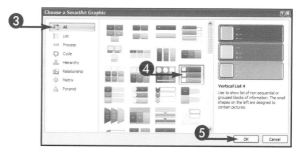

Excel adds the graphic to your worksheet and displays the Type Your Text Here dialog box.

⑥ Type text into the dialog box.

⑦ Click outside the chart to view it.

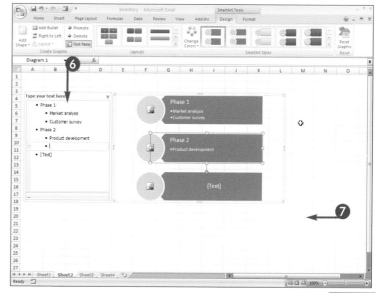

Analyzing Worksheet Data

You can organize large lists of data in Excel by creating database tables. This chapter shows you how to build a database, add records, sort and filter data, and perform a detailed analysis on the data using PivotTables.

Understanding Database Lists

You can use Excel as a database program to organize, sort, filter, and analyze lists of data. A database is a collection of related information. For example, an address book is a database list of names and addresses of your contacts. A television guide is also an example of a database, listing television programs, channels, and air times. You can create a variety of database lists in Excel to manage sales contacts, inventory, household valuables, and more.

Fields

You use *fields* to break down your database list into manageable pieces. In Excel, fields are typically the columns you use to define each part of your list. For example, an address database includes fields such as name, address, and phone number. Field names, also called *labels*, appear at the top of a list.

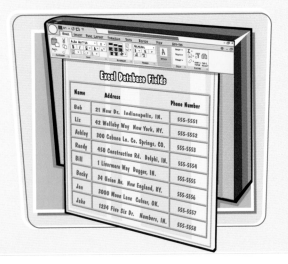

Records

You use rows to enter each database entry for your list of data. Database entries are called *records*. For example, in an inventory database, a single row contains all the information about an item in the inventory. Each row represents one record in the database.

Tables

An entire database list of information is called a *table*. You can create multiple tables in Excel. For example, one table might list customers and addresses, and another might list product items and prices. You might pull information from two tables to create a third table, such as a table listing customers and the items they buy.

Forms

You can use a *Data Form* to speed up the task of entering records into a database list. In Excel, the Data Form is a special dialog box consisting of all the fields in your table. To enter a record, you can fill out the form fields.

Plan a Database

Before you create a database list in Excel, take time to plan it out. Planning beforehand can alleviate having to reorganize your database later when you discover you left out important fields. Start by determining what kind of data you want to store and how it should be organized. Decide in what order you want to enter data. Each database table should have a specific topic, such as product inventory or client addresses. Most databases are comprised of at least two or more fields or columns.

Database Tips

Do not include blank rows in a database table. For best results, break out data into separate fields. For example, break City and State into two separate fields, instead of combining them into one. This can help you perform better analysis tasks later. It is not a good idea to place multiple tables on a single sheet; instead, place each one on a separate sheet in the workbook file.

Create a Database Table

You can use an Excel worksheet to build a database to manage large lists of data. A database is simply a collection of related records, such as a phone directory, address list, inventory, and so on. After creating a database table, you can perform a variety of analysis, sorting, and filtering techniques on the data.

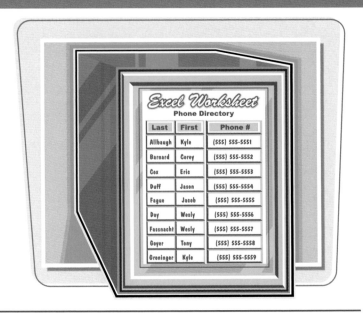

Create a Database Table

Type Field Labels

1. Click where you want to insert the first column.

2. Type a field label.

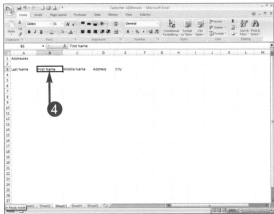

3. Press **Tab**.

4. Type the next field label.

5. Repeat steps **3** and **4** to continue entering as many field labels as your list requires.

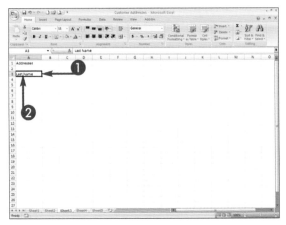

Enter Records

① Click in the first row beneath the field labels.

② Type the data for the first field.

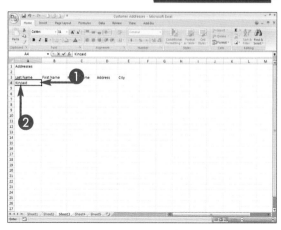

③ Press Tab.

④ Type the next field data.

⑤ Repeat steps **3** and **4** to continue filling in a complete record.

⑥ Press Enter.

● Excel starts a new record for the table by moving automatically to the next row.

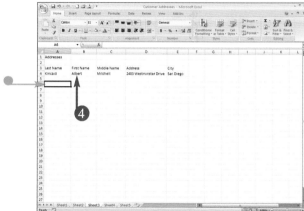

How do I quickly fill in records for my table?

Entering data into a table can be tedious. To speed up the task, you can use Excel's PickList feature. PickList is activated as soon as you create the first record in your table. It remembers the previous field entries so you can repeat them, if necessary. Follow these steps to use PickList:

① Right-click the cell in the new record.

② Click **Pick From Drop-down List**.

A list of previous entries appears.

③ Click an entry to repeat it in the current cell.

You can also press Enter or Tab to accept the entry, or press Esc to cancel.

continued

Create a Database Table *(continued)*

All database lists, also called *tables*, are built of fields and records. After entering records into your table, you can turn the data into a database list. Excel automatically adds filter arrows to each field label, allowing for quick filtering tasks.

You cannot create a database table in a shared workbook. To learn more about shared workbooks, see Chapter 13.

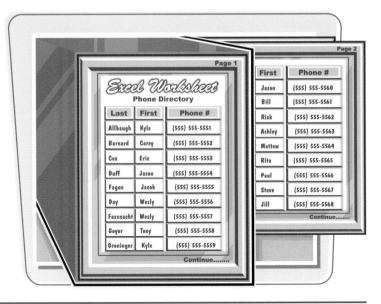

Page 1

Page 2

Create a Database Table *(continued)*

⑦ Repeat steps **2** to **6** to continue entering records for your table.

Create a Table

① Select the data you want to turn into a database table.

② Click the **Insert** tab.

③ Click **Table**.

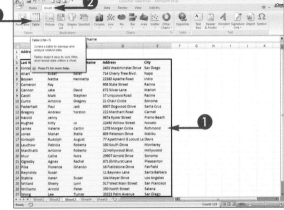

The Create Table dialog box opens.

● By default, the selected range appears here. If the range is not correct, you can select the correct cell references.

● Select this option (☐ changes to ☑) if necessary to include the headers in your table.

④ Click **OK**.

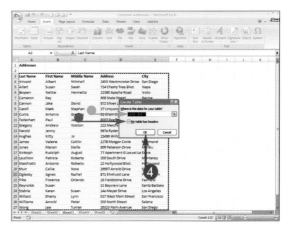

● Excel turns the data into a table, fills the cells of the table with blue shading, and displays filter arrows (▾) for each field.

The Table Tools Design tab also appears on-screen.

● To filter a list, click ▾ and click the data you want to filter out.

Note: *Learn more about Excel's AutoFilter feature in the section "Filter Data with AutoFilter," later in this chapter.*

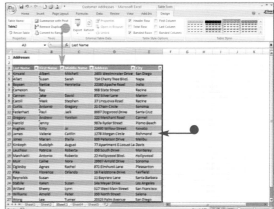

TIPS

Do I have to turn my data into a table?

No. You can still treat your data as a database without having to turn it into an official Excel table. The advantage to the Create Table command is that it automatically adds ▾ to your field labels. You can also sort by ascending or descending order from the AutoFilter drop-down lists. To learn more about filtering data, see the section "Filter Data with AutoFilter."

Can I turn my list back into a regular range?

Yes. To convert the list back to a regular Excel range, select the list, click **the Table Tools Design tab**, and then click **Convert to Range**. Click **Yes** when prompted. Excel removes the AutoFilter arrows from the field labels. You can still treat the data as a database, performing sorts and filters, even without the official list status.

Add Records Using a Data Form

Another way to enter database records is to use Excel's Data Form. The Data Form is a handy dialog box you can use to type the data for each field in your table, one record at a time. You are less likely to enter wrong information into a field when using a form than when directly entering data into your worksheet cells.

The command to display the data form is not located on the ribbon. You have to go to Excel Options in the File menu, and from the Customization page's Commands Not in the Ribbon list, add the Form command to the Quick Access Toolbar. See Chapter 1 to see how to do this.

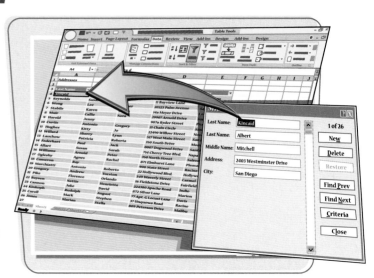

Add Records Using a Data Form

① Enter a record in a row.

② Select the first cell of a record.

③ Click **Form** on the Quick Access toolbar.

*Note: If your database has no records yet, a prompt box appears. Click **OK** to continue.*

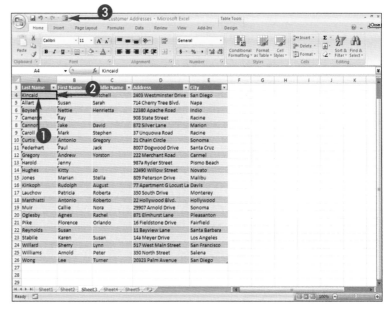

The data entry dialog box opens.

④ Click **New**.

5 Type the data for the first field.

6 Press **Tab**.

7 Repeat steps **3** to **4** to continue filling in form fields.

● You can click **New** to enter another record.

8 Click **Close**.

● Excel adds the record or records to the database list.

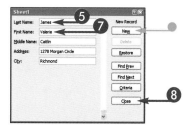

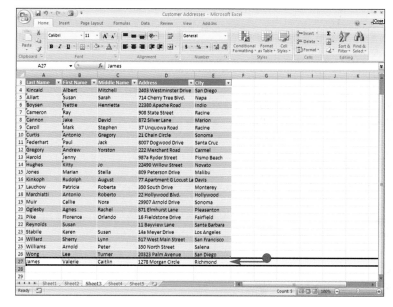

 TIPS

How do I navigate through my records using a form?

You can use the Data Form dialog box to navigate between all the records in your table. Click **Find Prev** to move backward through the table, or click **Find Next** to move forward. Any time you want to add a new record, click **New** and fill out the fields.

What methods can I use to delete a record?

You can open the Data Form dialog box and navigate to the record. Click the **Delete** button and confirm the deletion, and the record is gone. You can also click and drag your mouse across the fields of the record in the table on the Excel worksheet and then press Delete.

Edit Records

You can edit your database table by making changes to the records. For example, you might need to change a record's details or delete a record you no longer need. You can edit cells, columns, and rows directly in the table, or you can use the Data Form dialog box to make changes, as shown in this section.

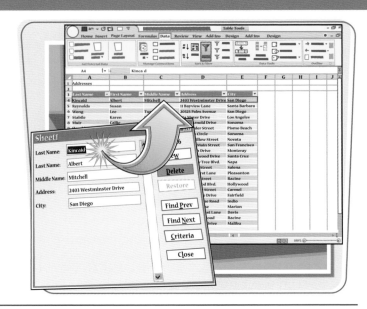

Edit Records

Change a Record

① Click anywhere in the table and then click **Form** on the Quick Access toolbar.

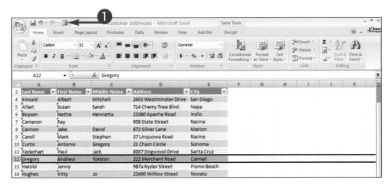

The Data Form dialog box opens.

② Scroll to locate the record you want to edit.

③ Click in the field you want to edit and then make your changes.

You can double-click a field to highlight all the data.

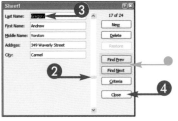

● Click **Find Prev** or **Find Next** to navigate to the next record you want to change.

④ Click **Close**.

The record or records are changed.

Delete a Record

1 Open the Data Form dialog box.

Note: *See the previous steps to learn how to open the dialog box.*

2 Click **Find Prev** or **Find Next** to navigate to the record you want to remove.

3 Click **Delete**.

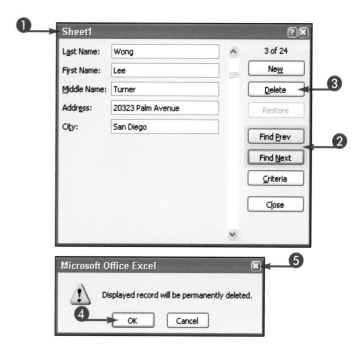

A prompt box appears warning about the deletion.

4 Click **OK**.

5 Click the **Close** button (⊠).

The record is deleted.

TIPS

How do I add a new record using the form?

To add a new record at any time, click **New**. The Data Form dialog box immediately displays a new record, and you can start typing new data into the fields.

What does the Restore button do?

You can click **Restore** to undo the previous action. For example, if you just typed data into a field, clicking **Restore** immediately removes the data.

Search for Records

You can use the Data Form to help you display only records matching the criteria you specify. For example, if you want to view all the clients from the same city or state, you can use the Data Form to search for matching records.

Search for Records

1 Open the Data Form dialog box.

Note: *You can click* **Form** *on the Quick Access toolbar to open the form. See the section "Add Records Using a Data Form" to learn more about using the Data Form dialog box.*

2 Click **Criteria**.

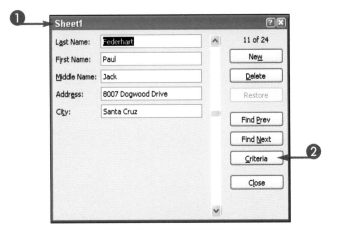

3 Click in the field for which you want to specify search criteria and then type the criteria you want to match.

4 Click **Find Prev** or **Find Next** to navigate through the matches.

● When you finish searching through records, click **Close** to close the form.

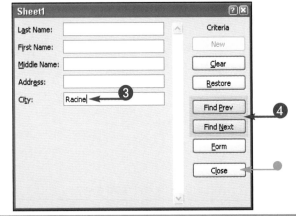

You can quickly find and remove duplicate records in a database using the Remove Duplicates button. This feature helps you keep your database current.

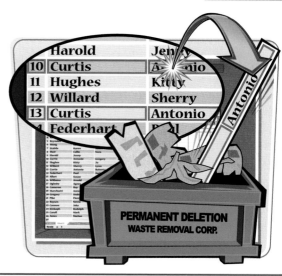

Identify Duplicate Values in a Table

1 Click anywhere in the table.

2 Click the **Table Tools Design** tab.

3 Click **Remove Duplicates**.

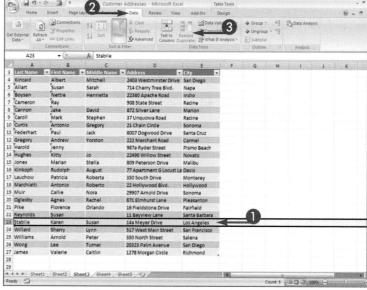

The Remove Duplicates dialog box appears.

4 Click (☑ changes to ☐) to deselect any field for which you do not want to remove duplicates.

5 Click **OK**.

A message appears reporting how many duplicate records were removed.

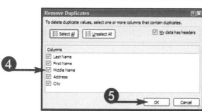

Set Data Validation Rules

You can set up your database table to control exactly what kinds of data are allowed in the cells. This is handy if other people use your list to enter records. You can make sure that they type the right kind of data in a cell by assigning a data validation rule. If they type the wrong data, such as text data instead of numerical data, Excel displays an error box to prompt them about what data can be entered into the cell.

Set Data Validation Rules

① Select the range to which you want to apply a data validation rule.

② Click the **Data** tab.

③ Click **Data Validation**.

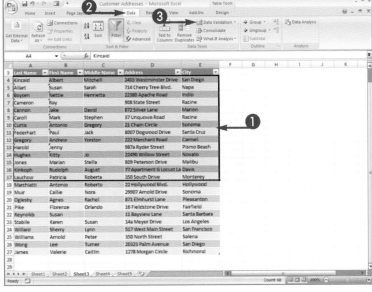

The Data Validation dialog box opens.

④ Click the **Settings** tab.

⑤ Click here and then select which type of data you want the cell to allow.

⑥ Define the data type parameters, if needed, by clicking the **Collapse** button (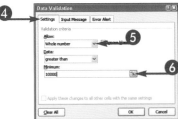).

7 Click the **Error Alert** tab.

8 Type a title for the error message.

9 Type instructions to help the user remedy the mistake.

10 Click **OK**.

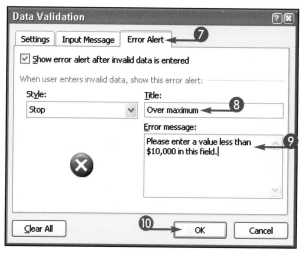

- If you or another user type the wrong data in the table's cells, an error alert box appears.

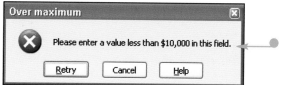

TIPS

What does the Input Message tab do?

You can include an input box that helps users know what data to type when they select a cell. The input box appears when a user selects a cell in the range. To add an input box, click the **Input Message** tab in the Data Validation dialog box and then enter an input title and message.

How do I turn off Data Validation?

To remove data validation, select the range containing the data validation rule and then reopen the Data Validation dialog box. Click **Clear All**. This turns off the data validation rules.

Sort Records

You can sort your database table to reorganize the information. For example, you might want to sort a client table to list the names alphabetically. An ascending sort lists records from A to Z, and a descending sort lists records from Z to A.

Sort Records

Perform a Quick Sort

① Click in the field name you want to sort.

② Click the **Data** tab.

③ Click **Sort A to Z** (图) or **Sort Z to A** (图).

You can also click 🔽 and choose sort commands from the menu that appears.

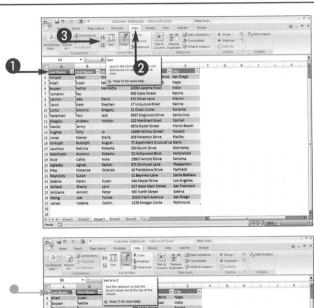

● Excel sorts the records based on the field you specified.

Note: If you do not want the records sorted permanently, click 🔄 to return the list to its original state.

Sort with the Sort Dialog Box

1 Click the **Data** tab.

2 Click **Sort**.

The Sort dialog box opens.

3 Click here and then select the primary field to sort by.

4 Click whether you want to sort the field in ascending or descending order.

● To specify additional fields for the sort, choose criteria from the Sort on drop-down list.

5 To add additional sort levels, click **Add Level** and then make settings for the next sort level.

6 Click **OK**.

Excel sorts the data.

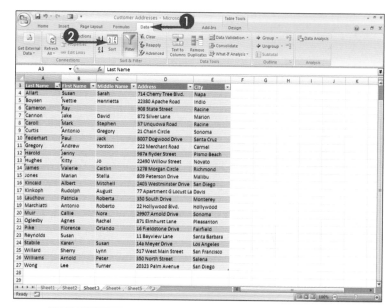

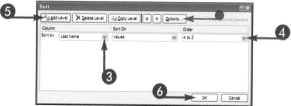

Can I sort data in rows?

Yes. If the listed data is across a row instead of down a column, you can activate the **Sort left to right** option in the Sort dialog box. Follow these steps:

1 Open the Sort dialog box using the steps in this section.

2 Click **Options**.

The Sort Options dialog box opens.

3 Click the **Sort left to right** option (○ changes to ◉).

4 Click **OK**.

Excel sorts your data.

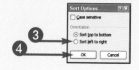

Filter Data with AutoFilter

You can use a filter to view only portions of your data. Unlike a sort, which sorts the entire table, a filter selects certain records to display based on your criteria, while hiding the other records that do not match the criteria.

Filter Data with AutoFilter

1 Select the field labels for the data you want to filter.

2 Click the **Data** tab.

3 Click **Filter**.

If you used the Create Table command to create a database table, your table already displays the AutoFilter buttons.

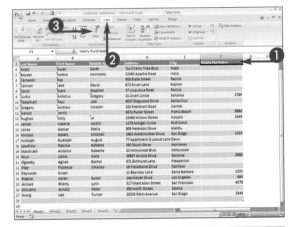

● Excel adds ▼ to your field labels.

4 Click ▼.

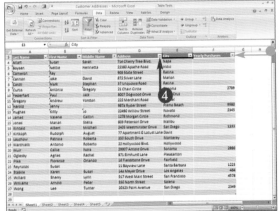

⑤ Click any item you want filtered out
(☑ changes to ☐).

Records that match the checked items
remain after you apply the filter.

⑥ Click **OK**.

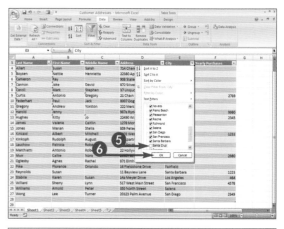

● Excel filters the table and replaces the filter
arrow with a filter icon.

To view all the records again, display the
filter list and click **Clear Filter from
"Field Name."**

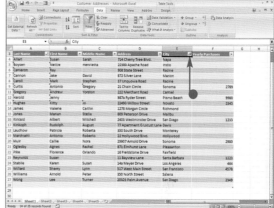

TIPS

**If I clear a filter, is
there a quick way to
get it back?**

If you have just cleared
the filter and want
to see it again, you
can click the
Reapply button on
the Data tab of the
ribbon.

**In what ways can I customize a
filter?**

You can activate the **Advanced** command
on the Data tab to open the
Advanced Filter dialog
box. Here you can
further customize the
filter by selecting
operators and
values to apply on
the filtered data. To
learn more about
customizing
AutoFilters, see
Excel's Help files.

Filter Criteria

✓Salespeople A-H
✓Sales over $50,000
✓Sales in New York
✓Sales during May
✓Sales for Export

Analyze Data with a PivotTable

You can use PivotTables to gain different perspectives on your data. PivotTables enable you to ask certain questions of your data to help you see beyond the obvious. Rather than examining the data for answers yourself, a PivotTable helps you to quickly analyze the meaning of sets of data.

For example, say you have a sales order table that describes products, quantities ordered, dates, amounts, buyers, and salespersons. You can use a PivotTable to find out which salesperson has the most sales, which buyer buys the most product, what items are the top sellers, and who sold the most product on a given day. These are just a few analysis points you can find out with PivotTables.

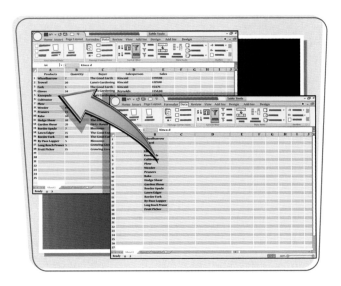

Analyze Data with a PivotTable

1. Click inside the database list.

2. Click the **Insert** tab.

3. Click **PivotTable**.

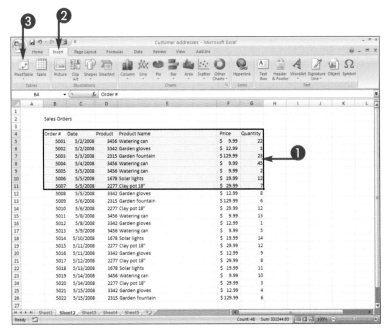

The Create Pivot Table dialog box opens.

4. Click 📇 to choose the table range.

5 Select a range and then click .

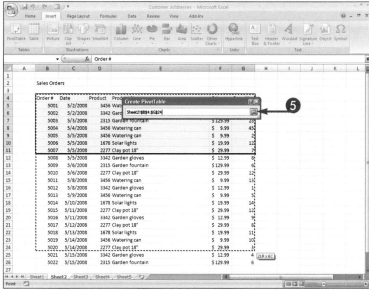

6 Click to specify where to place the table
(○ changes to ◉).

7 Click **OK**.

TIPS

Can I change any options for my PivotTable?

On the PivotTable Tools tab, you can click **Options** to display the PivotTable Options dialog box. Here you can modify the layout and format of the PivotTable, decide whether to show totals or filter data, and more.

How are PivotTables constructed?

PivotTables are made of row fields and column fields that summarize data across rows and fields, respectively. The middle area is where the actual analysis occurs for summarizing different fields of data pertaining to the row and column fields.

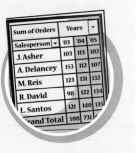

continued

After you create a PivotTable, you can drag various fields into the table to perform analyses. It might take some experimenting to figure out how your data works within the PivotTable. As you add and subtract fields and change their position on the table, the data you examine "pivots," hence the name *PivotTable*.

Any field you drag into the row area of the table becomes a row, and any field you drag into the column area becomes a column in the table. You can drag any field you want to summarize into the data area of the table. You can add multiple fields to the analysis.

Excel opens a new, empty PivotTable and displays the PivotTable Field List.

⑧ Click a field you want to analyze (☐ changes to ☑).

In this example, the PivotTable analyzes total price of sales.

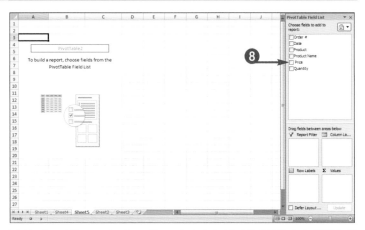

⑨ Drag the field box to the Column Label or Row Label area of the PivotTable Field List.

In this example, the PivotTable adds the quantity sold to the analysis.

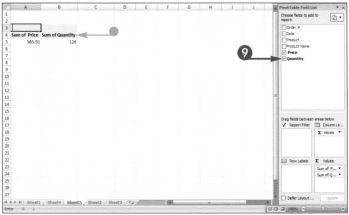

⑩ Click another field you want to analyze.

In this example, the PivotTable analyzes the dates of sales.

● Excel adds the field data, which you can then analyze.

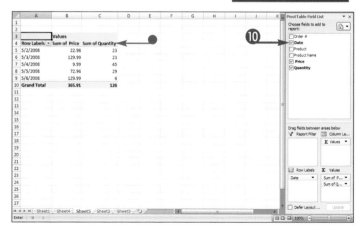

In this example, the PivotTable shows how many products were sold at a total price by date.

● To remove a field from the table, click the field to deselect it (☑ changes to ☐).

To add more fields to the mix, select them in the PivotTable Field List. You can also drag the fields from one area of the table to another.

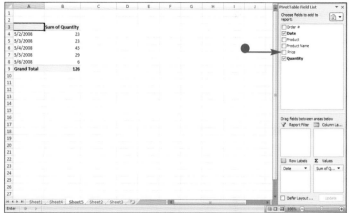

How do I change the summary function?

① Click the **PivotTable Tools Options** tab.

The PivotTable tab appears.

② Click **Field List**.

③ Click the **Values** ▼ and choose **Field Settings**.

The Data Field settings dialog box appears.

④ Click on any type of calculation for that field.

⑤ Click **OK**.

Using
Excel Tools

Excel offers a variety of special features and handy tools you can use to accomplish different tasks, such as speeding up your Excel work, analyzing data, and producing the results for which you are looking.

Add a Watch Window

You can use a Watch Window to keep track of data in a particular cell or range of cells even when the cells are no longer in view. This is especially useful if you want to keep your eye on a specific formula or the cells you use to create a formula. You might also use a Watch Window to keep track of a particular cell's data as you work with the rest of your worksheet.

Add a Watch Window

① Click the **Formulas** tab.

② Click **Watch Window**.

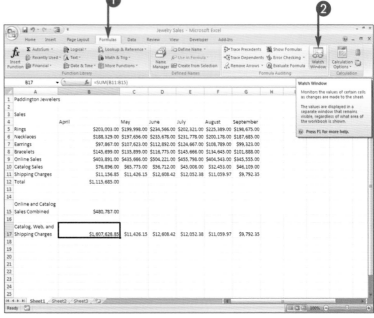

The Watch Window opens.

③ Click **Add Watch**.

④ Select the cell or cells you want to watch.

You can also type in the cell reference.

⑤ Click **Add**.

Note: You can add multiple cells to the Watch Window.

● Excel adds the cells to the Watch Window, including any values or formulas within the cells.

If you scroll away from the original cells, the Watch Window always displays the cell contents.

To return to the original cell, double-click the cell name.

⑥ Click the **Close** icon (☒).

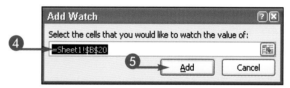

Add Watch

Select the cells that you would like to watch the value of:

④ =Sheet1!$B$20

⑤ → Add   Cancel

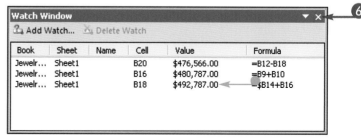

⑥

Watch Window   ▼ ✕

🔒 Add Watch...   🔓 Delete Watch

Book	Sheet	Name	Cell	Value	Formula
Jewelr...	Sheet1		B20	$476,566.00	=B12-B18
Jewelr...	Sheet1		B16	$480,787.00	=B9+B10
Jewelr...	Sheet1		B18	$492,787.00	◀— =$B14+B16

TIPS

How do I remove a cell from the Watch Window?

To remove a cell from the Watch Window, click the cell name and then click **Delete Watch**. Excel immediately removes the cell from the window.

Can I move the Watch Window?

Yes. To move the window, simply click and drag the window's title bar (◹ becomes ✛). You can reposition the window anywhere on-screen. You can also dock the window to appear with the toolbars at the top of the Excel program window. You can also resize the columns within the Watch Window. Position ◹ over a column in the Watch Window and drag to resize the column.

Load Add-Ins

Excel offers a variety of add-ins you can install. Add-ins are simply programs included with Excel to offer additional worksheet efficiency. By default, Excel does not install the add-ins until requested.

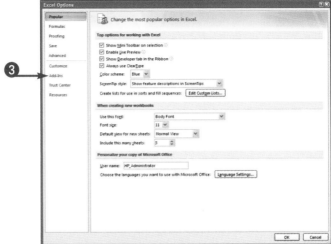

Load Add-Ins

① Click .

The File menu appears.

② Click **Excel Options**.

The Excel Options dialog box opens.

③ Click **Add-Ins**.

④ Click the **Manage** ▼ and choose a type of add-in.

⑤ Click **Go**.

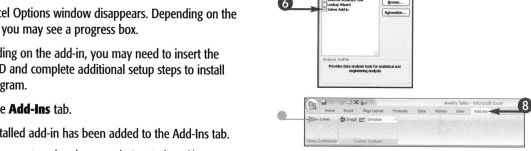

The Add-Ins dialog box opens.

⑥ Click to select an add-in (☐ changes to ☑).

⑦ Click **OK**.

The Excel Options window disappears. Depending on the add-in, you may see a progress box.

Depending on the add-in, you may need to insert the Excel CD and complete additional setup steps to install the program.

⑧ Click the **Add-Ins** tab.

● The installed add-in has been added to the Add-Ins tab.

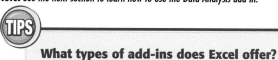

Note: See the next section to learn how to use the Data Analysis add-in.

TIPS

What types of add-ins does Excel offer?

The Excel Options window offers items in seven categories of add-ins that you can install, including the Analysis Toolpak, Analysis Toolpak VBA, Conditional Sum Wizard, Euro Currency Tools, Internet Assistant VBA, Lookup Wizard, and Solver Add-In. You can also find additional add-ins on the Microsoft Office Web site. To learn more about add-ins, consult the Excel Help files.

How do I unload an add-in?

You can unload any add-in you install. Unloading an add-in can free up memory as well as reduce the number of menu commands appearing on the Tools or Data menus. To unload an add-in, simply reopen the Add-In dialog box, choose the type of add-in in the Manage field, and in the resulting dialog box, deselect the program you no longer want to use (☑ changes to ☐). After unloading, the add-in program name disappears from the Add-Ins tab.

Analyze Data with Add-In Tools

If you need to perform more powerful statistical functions or engineering analyses, you can access Excel's Data Analysis tools. The Data Analysis tools include tools for random number generation, sampling, regression analysis, and more. With the Data Analysis tools, you provide the data from your worksheet and the tool provides the results.

The Analysis Toolpak is just one of several add-in programs you can install to work with Excel. To learn more about loading add-ins, see the previous section.

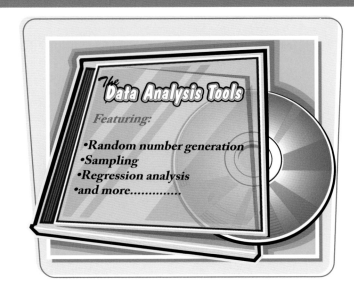

Using Data Analysis Tools

① Click the **Data** tab.

② Click **Data Analysis**.

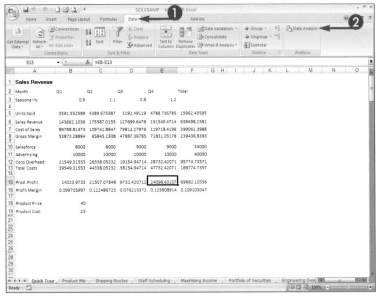

The Data Analysis dialog box opens.

③ Click the analysis tool you want to use.

● You can use the scroll bar to view all the available tools.

④ Click **OK**.

The tool's dialog box opens.

5 Select or type the input range to use in the analysis.

6 Select or type the output range to use in the analysis.

● You can select any additional options to apply to the tool (○ changes to ●).

7 Click **OK**.

● Excel executes the analysis tool.

In this example, the Sampling tool produces a random sampling of income values.

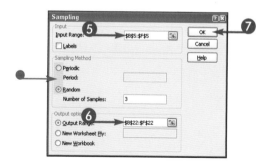

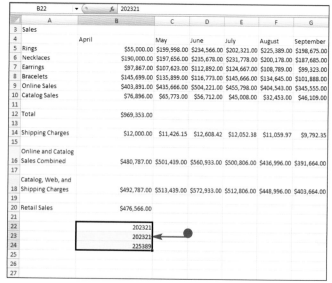

TIPS

Where can I learn more about each Data Analysis tool?

You can use Excel's Help files to learn how each tool works. In the Data Analysis dialog box, click **Help**. This opens the Excel Help window where you can search by any analysis type, such as sampling, and read more about the tool and any of its settings. To learn more about using Excel Help, see Chapter 1.

Why do I not see Data Analysis on the Formulas tab?

If you have not loaded the Analysis Toolpak add-in to Excel, the tool will not appear on the Formulas tab. Although other add-ins are accessed from the Add-in tab, the Data Analysis tools of the Toolpak are not.

Examine Alternatives with Goal Seek

Goal Seek is one of several "what if" analysis tools you can use in Excel. You can use Excel's Goal Seek tool to work backward to a desired result and analyze what happens when you change values along the way. For example, if you are trying to calculate how much you can afford to spend each month on a new car purchase, Goal Seek can help you determine the loan amount.

In order to use Goal Seek, you must have at least one input cell that affects the value of the cell containing your goal.

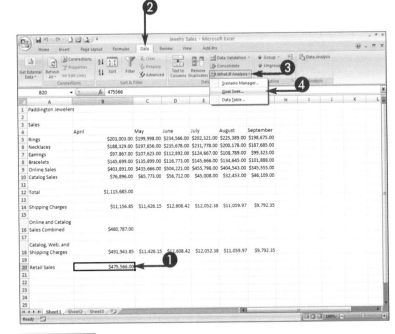

Using Goal Seek

1 Click the cell containing the goal you want to change.

2 Click the **Data** tab.

3 Click **What-If Analysis**.

4 Click **Goal Seek**.

The Goal Seek dialog box opens.

● The Set cell value is already filled in with the cell contents you selected in step **1**.

5 Type your goal value.

In this example, Goal Seek determines how much more income you need to receive for one product line to bring your total sales to a certain figure.

6 Select or type the cell reference you want to change to reach your goal value.

In this example, the loan amount is the amount that needs to change to reach the goal value.

7 Click **OK**.

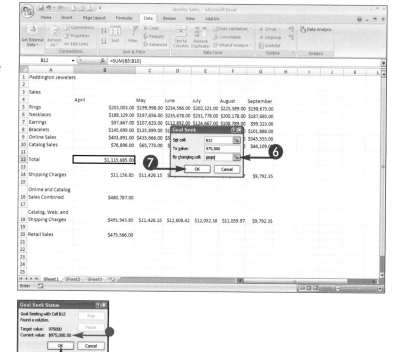

● Goal Seek produces a value change to meet your goal.

In this example, Goal Seek determines that the total sales in cell B20 can reach the desired goal by increasing sales of rings by an amount specified in cell B5.

8 Click **OK**.

Excel closes the Goal Seek Status box.

TIPS

What other ways can I use the Goal Seek tool?

You can use Goal Seek to help you solve single-variable equations of any kind. One of the most popular uses of Goal Seek is figuring out loan amounts and payments. You can also use Goal Seek to help you figure out how much you need to sell to reach a sales goal or how many units you have to sell to break even.

What tool can I use to figure out more complex goals?

Use Goal Seek when you want to produce a specific value by adjusting one input cell that influences the value. If you require more than one input cell, use Excel's Solver tool instead. Solver is an add-in you can use for complex problems that use multiple variables. Solver is very similar to Goal Seek. See the section "Optimizing Formulas with Solver," later in this chapter, to learn more.

Create Scenarios

You can use Excel's scenarios to perform "what if" speculations on your data. For example, you might use a scenario to examine what would happen if you increased shipping prices or raised product prices on your inventory worksheet. When you create a scenario, you make changes to the worksheet data without affecting the original data.

Create Scenarios

Create a Scenario

① Click the **Data** tab.

② Click **What-If Analysis**.

③ Click **Scenario Manager**.

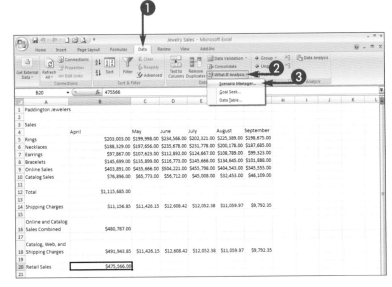

The Scenario Manager dialog box opens.

④ Click **Add**.

The Edit Scenario dialog box opens.

5 Type a name for the scenario.

6 Select the cells you want to change or type the cell references.

● You can click here to collapse () or expand (⬚) the dialog box while clicking cells in the worksheet.

● Optionally, you can type a note about the scenario here.

7 Click **OK**.

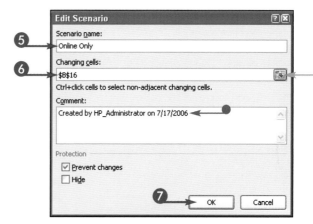

The Scenario Values dialog box opens.

8 Type values for each of the changing cells.

You can perform all kinds of changes to the data to create a scenario.

9 Click **OK**.

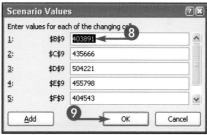

TIPS

Do I need to save my original worksheet data before creating scenarios?

Yes. Save the original worksheet data before using Excel's Scenario Manager. Because the Scenario Manager works by entering new values, any existing formulas are overwritten by new values you record in a scenario. You might also consider saving the original workbook using a new filename to further prevent any problems. To learn more about saving Excel workbooks, see Chapter 2.

Does the Scenario Manager store formulas along with cell contents?

No. Although the Scenario Manager does not store formulas, you can type them into the Scenario Values dialog box. For example, if you want to enter a value for cell G10 as 10 percent higher than the value in cell F10, you can type the formula **=F10*1.10** for the changing cell information for cell G10. Any results that are calculated are stored along with the scenario.

continued

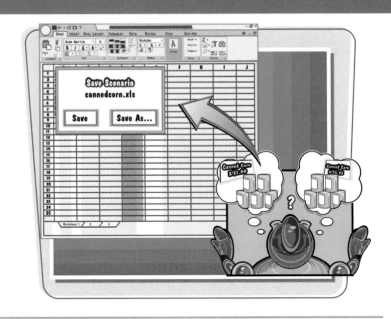

When you create scenarios, you save the scenario data to reuse again at a later time. The Scenario Manager dialog box keeps track of the workbook's scenarios, enabling you to revisit and make changes to the scenarios as needed.

Create Scenarios (continued)

You can continue adding more scenarios to Scenario Manager by repeating steps **3** to **9** earlier in this section.

⑩ Click **Close**.

Excel closes the Scenario Manager dialog box.

To view the newly created scenario, see the next set of steps; if Scenario Manager is already open, skip to step **4**.

View Scenarios

① Click **Data**.

② Click **What-If Analysis**.

③ Click **Scenario Manager**.

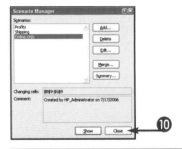

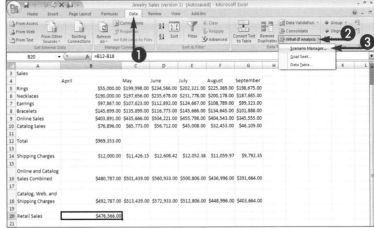

The Scenario Manager dialog box opens.

④ Click the scenario you want to view.

⑤ Click **Show**.

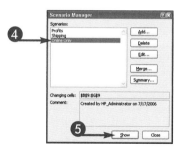

Excel displays the scenario on the worksheet.

● In this example, the scenario shows how sales revenue increases when product income and shipping revenue increase.

⑥ When finished viewing the scenario, click **Close**.

Excel closes the Scenario Manager dialog box; the last applied scenario remains in the worksheet.

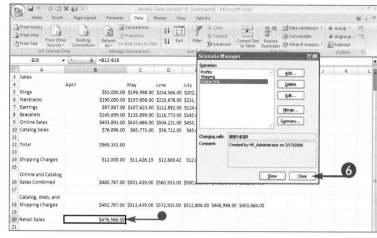

TIPS

How do I remove a scenario?

To remove a scenario you no longer want to keep, reopen the Scenario Manager dialog box (click **What-If Analysis** and then **Scenario Manager**). Click the scenario you want to remove and then click **Delete**. Scenario Manager permanently removes the scenario from the list.

What does the Summary button do in the Scenario Manager dialog box?

You can click **Summary** in the Scenario Manager to generate a summarization of your various scenarios. When activated, the Summary button opens the Scenario Summary dialog box, where you can create a report to list all the inputs and results for all the scenarios.

Optimize Formulas with Solver

Excel's Solver add-in can help you figure out a formula's optimal value using a group of related cells. To use Solver, you must first define the target cell, which is related to other cells through formulas. Solver analyzes the formulas used to create the target cell's answer and comes up with different solutions. You must also specify which changing cells Solver can modify to optimize the solution in the target cell.

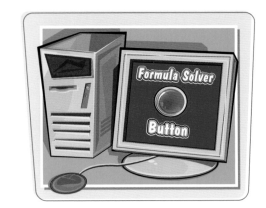

Solver works similarly to Excel's Goal Seek tool but offers more options. Solver is just one of several add-in programs that come with Excel. In order to use Solver, you must first load the add-in. See the section "Load Add-Ins" to learn how to install the tool.

Using Solver

① Click the **Add-Ins** tab.

② Click **Solver**.

Note: *If you have not yet loaded Solver, see "Load Add-Ins" to learn how.*

Note: *Excel installs with a sample workbook, named solvsamp.xls, which you can use to practice Solver problems. You can find the file using the path C:\Program Files\Microsoft Office\Office12\Samples.*

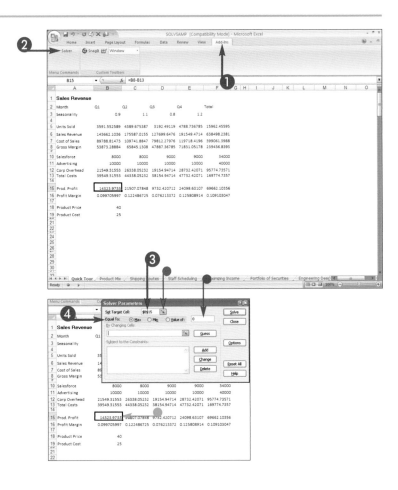

The Solver Parameters dialog box opens.

③ Type a cell reference for the target cell.

● You can also select a range directly on the worksheet.

● You can click here to collapse ([X]) or expand ([□]) the dialog box while clicking cells in the worksheet.

④ Click an **Equal To** option (○ changes to ⊙).

● If needed, type a value here.

⑤ Type a cell reference to compare against the target cell.

● You can also select a range directly on the worksheet.

To enter multiple non-contiguous cells, separate each cell reference with a comma.

⑥ Click **Solve**.

● You can click **Guess** to make Solver automatically propose adjustable cells based on the target cell.

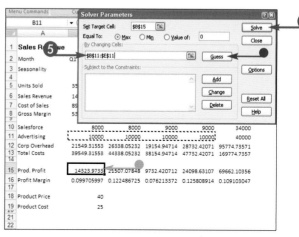

● The Solver Results dialog box opens, and Excel makes changes to the designated target cell.

⑦ Select whether you want to save the solution or restore to the original values (○ changes to ◉).

● If you click **Keep Solver Solution**, to save the results as a report, click a report type.

● To save the changes as a scenario, click here.

⑧ Click **OK**.

Excel closes the Solver Results dialog box.

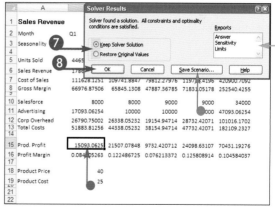

How do I define constraints for Solver?

Constraints limit what solutions Solver produces. Constraints are simply rules Solver must observe to produce the answers you want. For example, you can set constraints for the adjustable cells, the target cell, or any other cells related to the target cell. To add constraints to Solver, follow these steps:

① Per this section, open the Solver Parameters dialog box, defining the target and changing cells.

② Click **Add**.

③ In the Add Constraint dialog box, define one or more cell constraints.

④ Click **OK** to return to the Solver Parameters dialog box so you can run Solver.

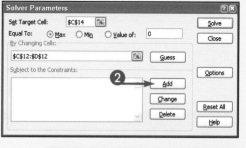

Sharing Excel Data

You can share Excel data between worksheets, workbooks, and with other users. This chapter shows you how to use a variety of data-sharing methods, including linking data, tracking multiple-user changes to workbook files, and e-mailing Excel data.

Link Data

You can use OLE technology to share data from your Excel worksheets. OLE stands for *object linking and embedding*. For example, you might link data from one workbook to another, or link Excel data to a Word or PowerPoint file.

Ordinarily, when you copy data, the data does not retain any connection to its source. With linking, the data retains a connection to its source, and any changes you make to the source data are immediately reflected in the linked data.

Link Data

① In the source file, select the data you want to link.

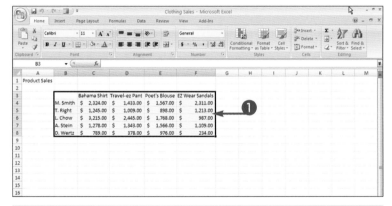

② Click the **Home** tab.

③ Click **Copy** (🖻).

You can also press Ctrl + C.

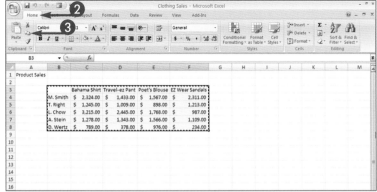

④ Open the destination file and click where you want to insert the copied data.

⑤ Click the **Home** tab.

⑥ Click **Paste** (📋).

⑦ Click **Paste Link.**

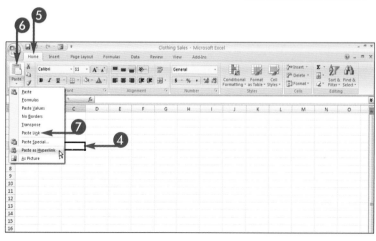

● Excel pastes the data into the worksheet.

Any changes you make to the source data are now reflected in the destination file.

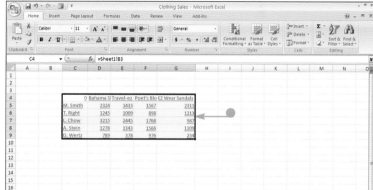

TIPS

What happens if I break a link?

If you move the source file to a new location or delete the source file, any links you have to the source data are broken. Broken links can also occur if you move the worksheet within the workbook. You can fix a link using the Edit Links dialog box. See the section "Edit Linked Data" to learn more.

What is the difference between linking data and embedding data?

Linked data always maintains a connection to the source data, and unless the link is broken, you can always count on the destination file being accurate because it is updated whenever the source data is updated. Embedded data maintains a connection to the program used to create the data. With embedded data, you do not have to worry about broken links; however, you have to update any changes to the data yourself.

Edit Linked Data

You can edit linked data using the Edit Links dialog box. This dialog box keeps track of all the links in a destination file and enables you to check link status, break links, and view the source data.

Edit Linked Data

① In the destination file, click the **Data** tab.

② Click **Edit Links to Files**.

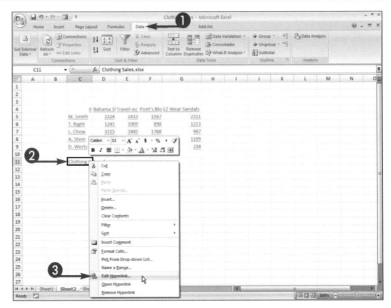

The Edit Links dialog box opens.

③ Click the link you want to edit.

④ Click an option.

You can update values, open and view the source data, change the source of your data, break a link, or check a link's status.

⑤ Click **OK**.

Excel edits the link.

You can link data between sheets using the Paste Options smart tag. When you create a link between sheets, any time you make changes to the source cells, the linked cells automatically reflect the new changes.

You can use this same technique to create links between Excel workbooks. The Paste Options smart tag appears immediately after you paste data. To learn more about working with smart tags, see Chapter 3.

Link Between Worksheets

① Select the cell or range you want to use as the source data.

② Click the **Home** tab.

③ Click 📋.

You can also press `Ctrl` + `C`.

④ Click the sheet tab to which you want to link.

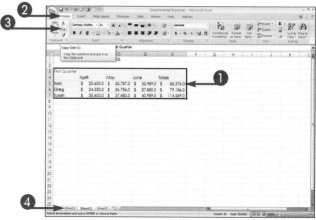

⑤ Click a cell or range for the pasted data.

⑥ Click the **Paste** icon (📋).

⑦ Click the **Paste Options smart tag** icon (📋).

⑧ Click the **Link Cells** option (○ changes to ◉).

Excel links the data.

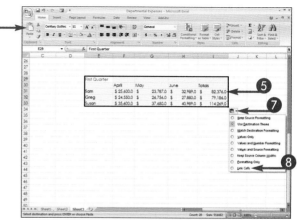

Embed Objects

You can use embedded objects to share data between files and programs. For example, you might embed a Word document or a PowerPoint slide in your Excel worksheet. With embedded data, you can make edits to the embedded object without leaving the destination program. Unlike linked data, which retains a direct link with the source data, embedded objects retain a connection with only the source program, not the source data.

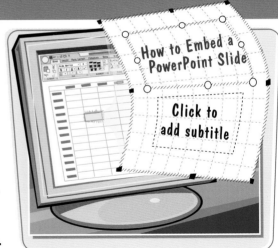

If the source object changes, the embedded object remains the same.

Embed Objects

1 Click where you want to insert the embedded object.

2 Click the **Insert** tab.

3 Click **Object**.

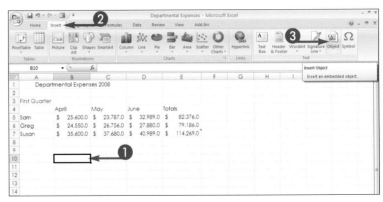

The Object dialog box opens.

4 Click the **Create New** tab.

5 Click the object type you want to embed.

6 Click **OK**.

Excel embeds the object and displays the source program's controls for you to create the new object.

In this example, PowerPoint's toolbars appear.

⑦ Create the new object using the source program's controls.

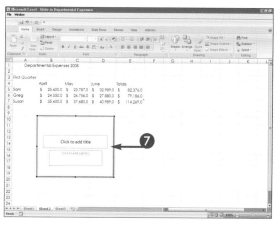

⑧ Click anywhere outside the object.

Excel's program controls reappear.

● To edit the object at any time, simply double-click the object and use the source program's controls to make changes.

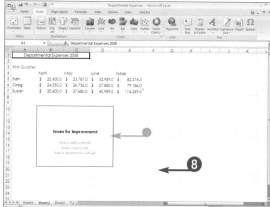

TIP

How do I embed an existing object?

If you already have an object you want to embed in a worksheet, you can use the Object dialog box to locate and embed the object. Follow these steps:

① Open the Object dialog box as shown in this section and click the **Create from File** tab.

② Click **Browse**.

● If you know the path to the file, you can type it here.

③ In the Browse dialog box that appears, double-click the file you want to embed and click **OK**.

④ Click **OK** to exit the dialog box and embed the object.

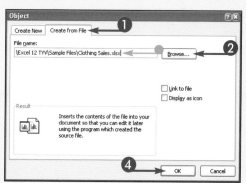

Enable Workbook Sharing

If you plan to share your workbooks with other users on a network, you can enable Excel's workbook-sharing feature. Sharing workbooks enables multiple users to edit a workbook simultaneously.

You can also track and review changes made to shared workbooks. See the section "Track and Review Workbook Changes" to learn more.

Enable Workbook Sharing

① Click the **Review** tab.

② Click **Share Workbook**.

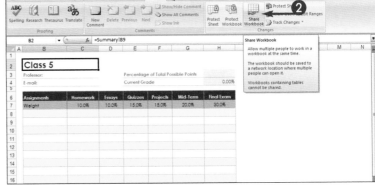

The Share Workbook dialog box opens.

③ Click the **Editing** tab.

④ Click **Allow changes by more than one user at the same time**
  (☐ changes to ☑).

⑤ Click **OK**.

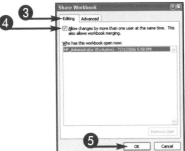

Excel prompts you to save the workbook.

Note: *Be sure to save the workbook to a network location or a shared network folder so others can find and use the file.*

6 Click **OK**.

If you have not previously saved the file, the Save As dialog box may appear. Save the file.

● Excel saves the workbook and adds the word *Shared* to the title bar.

You or other users can now make changes to the workbook.

Note: *See the section "Merge Workbooks" to learn how to merge changes.*

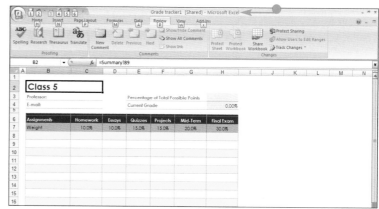

How do I change sharing options?

You can use the Advanced tab in the Share Workbook dialog box to set controls for how long Excel keeps track of changes and how often the file updates. You can also control what Excel does to resolve conflicts when two users change the same cells. Follow these steps to set up sharing options:

1 Open the Share Workbook dialog box as shown in this section.

2 Click the **Advanced** tab.

3 Select any sharing options you want to apply.

4 Click **OK**.

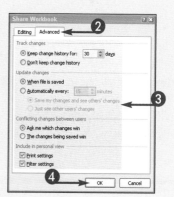

Add a Comment

You can add comments to your worksheets to make a note to yourself or to other users about a particular cell's contents. For example, if you share your workbooks with other users, you can add comments to leave feedback about the data without typing directly in the worksheet. Excel displays comments in a balloon.

Add a Comment

Add a Comment

① Click the cell to which you want to add a comment.

② Click the **Review** tab.

③ Click **New Comment**.

You can also right-click the cell and click **New Comment**.

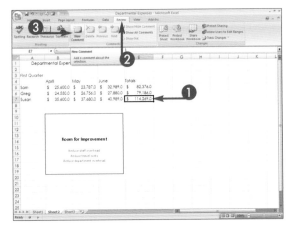

A comment balloon appears.

④ Type your comment text.

⑤ Click anywhere outside the comment balloon to deselect the comment.

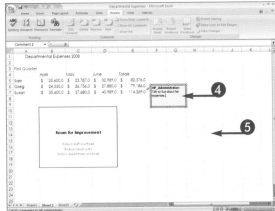

● Comment cells display a small red triangle (▾) in the corner.

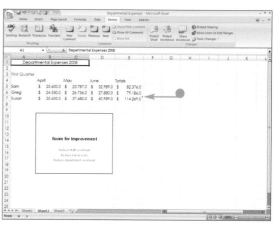

View a Comment

① Position the mouse pointer over the upper-right corner of the cell.

The comment balloon appears displaying the comment.

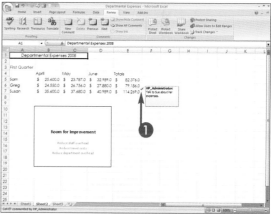

 TIPS

How do I remove a comment?

You can remove comments you no longer want to associate with a cell. Right-click the cell containing the comment to display a shortcut menu. Click **Delete Comment**. Excel immediately removes the comment from the cell.

How do I respond to another user's comment?

If the worksheet's tracking features are turned on, you can add a comment to another user's comment. Excel's tracking features enable you to see the edits each user makes to the workbook. After all the edits are complete, you can decide which edits to accept or reject to create a final file. To turn on workbook tracking, click **Review**, click **Track Changes**, and then click **Highlight Changes**. See the next section, "Track and Review Workbook Changes," to learn more.

Track and Review Workbook Changes

If you work in an environment in which you share your Excel workbooks with others, you can use the tracking and reviewing features to help you keep track of who adds changes to the file. For example, you can see what edits others have made, including formatting changes and data additions or deletions.

The tracking feature changes the color for each person's edits, making it easy to see who changed what in the workbook. When you review the workbook, you can choose to accept or reject the changes.

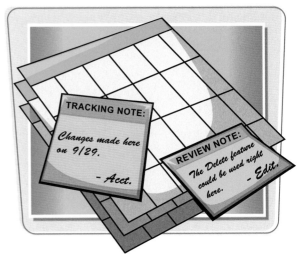

Track and Review Workbook Changes

Turn on Tracking

① Click the **Review** tab.

② Click **Track Changes**.

③ Click **Highlight Changes**.

The Highlight Changes dialog box opens.

④ Click **Track changes while editing**
(☐ changes to ☑).

This option automatically creates a shared workbook file if you have not already activated the Share Workbook feature.

● You can choose when, who, or where you track changes clicking these options.

● Leave this option selected to view changes in the file.

⑤ Click **OK**.

The Save As dialog box opens so you can save the changes.

⑥ Click **Save**.

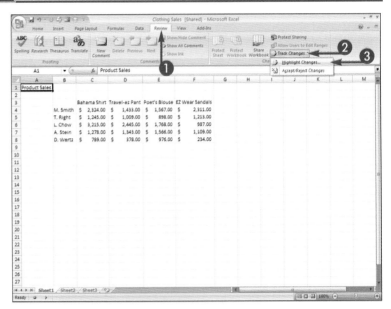

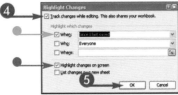

Excel's tracking feature is activated.

- Excel highlights any changes in the worksheet.
- To view details about a change and the author, position ⇖ over the highlighted cell.

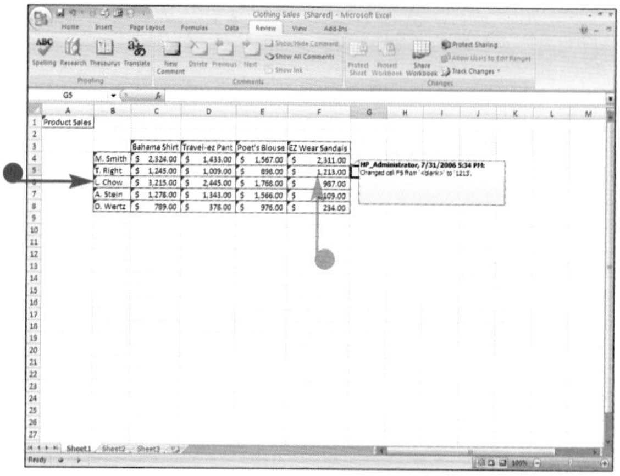

Review Changes

1. Click the **Review** tab.
2. Click **Track Changes**.
3. Click **Accept/Reject Changes**.

Excel prompts you to save the workbook if you have not already saved it.

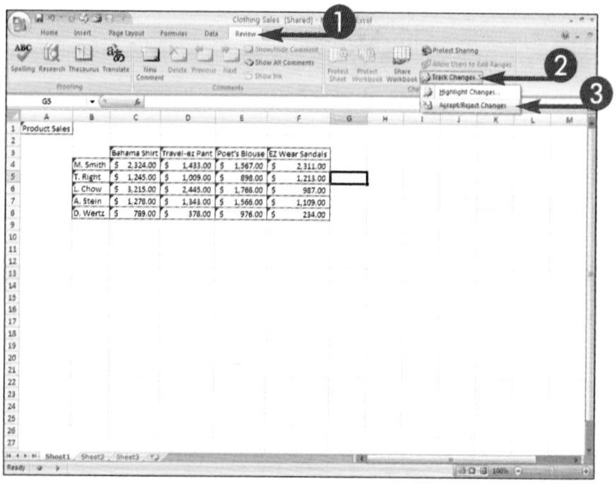

TIP

Is there a way to view all the changes at once when reviewing a workbook?

Yes. When you display the Highlight Changes dialog box (click **Review**, click **Track Changes,** and then click **Highlight Changes**), you can activate the List changes on a new sheet option. This opens a special History sheet in the workbook for viewing each edit. The History sheet breaks out the details of each edit, including the author, date, and time. You can use the filters to change the list of edits. When you save the workbook, the History sheet is deleted.

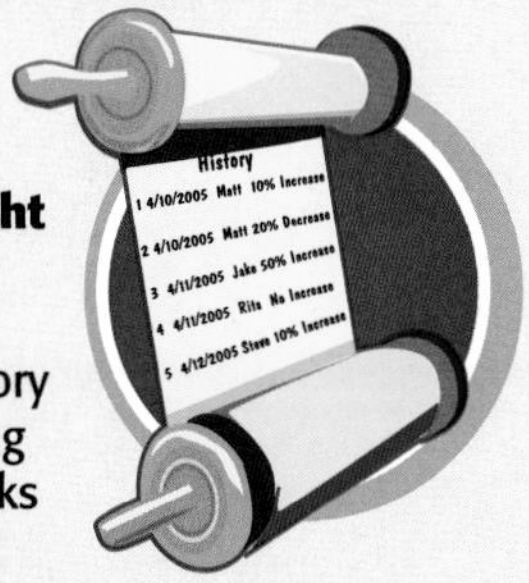

continued

After you activate the reviewing process, Excel goes through each change in the worksheet and enables you to accept or reject the edit. When the review is complete, you can turn the tracking feature off.

Track and Review Workbook Changes *(continued)*

The Select Changes to Accept or Reject dialog box opens.

④ Click which changes you want to view (☐ changes to ☑).

⑤ Click **OK**.

The Accept or Reject Changes dialog box opens, and Excel highlights the first change in the worksheet.

⑥ Specify an action for each edit.

You can click **Accept** to add the change to the final worksheet.

To reject the change, you can click **Reject**.

You can click **Accept All** or **Reject All** to accept or reject all the changes at once.

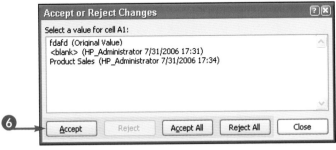

Turn Off Tracking

1 Click the **Review** tab.

2 Click **Track Changes**.

3 Click **Highlight Changes**.

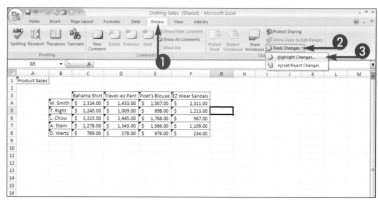

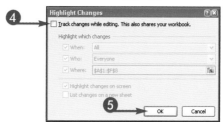

The Highlight Changes dialog box opens.

4 Click **Track changes while editing**
(☑ changes to ☐) to deselect the option.

5 Click **OK**.

Excel's tracking feature is turned off. If you have shared this workbook, a message appears that this action removes this workbook from shared use. Click **OK**.

Are there certain edits Excel does not track or highlight?

Excel's tracking feature does not keep track of changes in sheet names, inserted or deleted sheets, or hidden rows or columns. In addition, some of Excel's features do not work with shared workbooks, such as grouping data, recording and assigning macros, or inserting pictures or hyperlinks. For a complete list of changes and features supported with shared workbooks, see Excel's Help files.

Can I remove a user from a shared workbook?

Yes. You can open the Share Workbook dialog box and view which users are using the file. See the section "Enable Workbook Sharing" to learn how to access the dialog box. You can then remove users by clicking their names and clicking **Remove User**.

Merge Workbooks

You can merge shared workbooks to create a single final file incorporating every user's input. For example, if each user saves the same file with a different name, you can incorporate all the versions of the file into one workbook to include everyone's edits to the data. To merge workbooks, make sure all the workbooks are stored in the same folder.

Merge Workbooks

① Add the Compare and Merge Workbooks command to the Quick Access toolbar by selecting it from the Commands Not Shown on Ribbon category.

Note: See Chapter 1 for more about customizing the Quick Access toolbar.

② Click **Compare and Merge Workbooks**.

Note: This feature is available only in shared workbooks. See the section "Enable Workbook Sharing" to learn more.

Excel might prompt you to save the workbook.

③ Click **OK**.

The Select Files to Merge into Current Workbook dialog box opens.

④ Navigate to the folder containing the workbooks you want to merge.

5 Click the filenames you want to merge.

To click multiple files, press and hold Ctrl while clicking filenames.

6 Click **OK**.

Excel merges all the workbooks into one.

● In this example, other users' input is incorporated into the workbook.

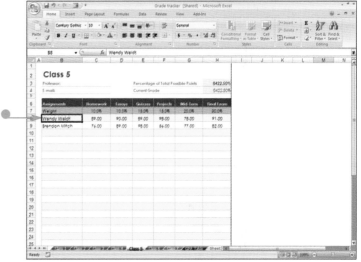

TIP

How do I turn off workbook sharing?

To turn off workbook sharing, follow these steps:

1 Open the Share Workbook dialog box (click **Review**, and then click **Share Workbook**).

2 Deselect the **Allow changes by more than one user at the same time** option (☑ changes to ☐).

3 Click **OK**.

Excel turns off the sharing feature.

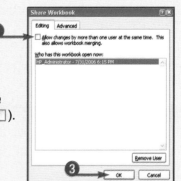

E-mail a Workbook

You can e-mail a workbook without leaving the Excel program window. For example, you might want to send the workbook to a colleague for review. Most e-mail editors, including Outlook Express and Office Live Mail, allow you to tap into features to insert e-mail addresses and send an Excel workbook as an e-mail message.

You might need to log on to your Internet account before sending an e-mail message from Excel.

E-mail a Workbook

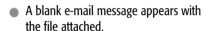

① Click 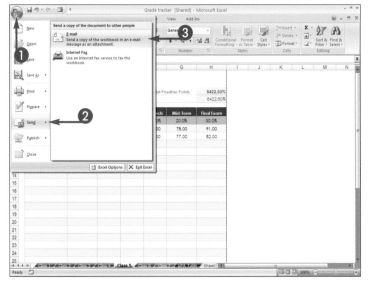.

② Click **Send**.

③ Click **E-mail**.

● A blank e-mail message appears with the file attached.

④ Type the recipient's e-mail address.

● If you are using Outlook or Outlook Express you can click the **To** button to access the Outlook Address Book and retrieve an address.

If typing more than one e-mail address, use a semicolon to separate them.

⑤ You can change the subject title for the message.

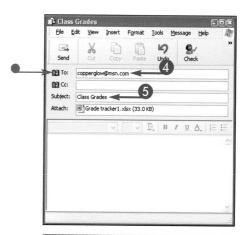

● Optionally, you can type a brief message here.

● You can use the e-mail program controls to format your message.

⑥ Click **Send**.

The message is sent to your Outbox ready for e-mailing.

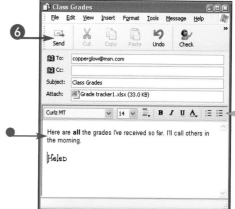

TIP

If I send the workbook as an e-mail attachment, can the recipient make changes and send it back?

Yes. When users receive the attachment, they can review the file, add their own changes, and e-mail the file back to you.

ATTACHMENT
To:
jim@abc.net

Import Data

You can transfer data from other sources into your Excel worksheet. For example, you can import text files as well as database and Web queries.

Import Data

1 Click the **Data** tab.

2 Click **Get External Data**.

3 Click **From Text**.

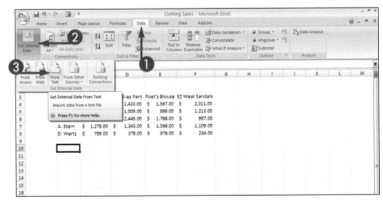

The Import Text File dialog box opens.

4 Navigate to the file you want to import.

5 Click the filename.

6 Click **Import**.

Excel imports the data.

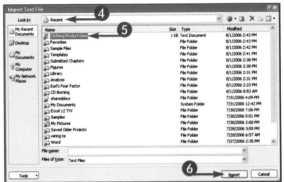

You can use the Save As dialog box to export your workbook data by saving the data as another file format. For example, you might save your workbook as a text file to send to someone who does not use Excel as his or her spreadsheet program.

Export Data

1 Click .

2 Click **Save As**.

The Save As dialog box opens.

3 Navigate to the folder to which you want to save the file.

4 Type a filename.

5 Click the Save as Type ☐ and select a file type.

6 Click **Save**.

Excel saves the data to the new format.

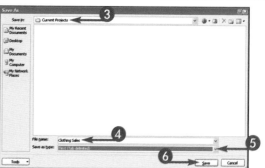

Using Excel on the Web

Excel offers several tools you can use to turn your worksheet data into Web pages. You can also view Web pages, turn Web content into worksheet data, and download the latest stock quotes. This chapter shows you how to incorporate Web tasks into your worksheets.

Add Web Tools to the Quick Access Toolbar

The Quick Access Toolbar contains three tools by default: Save, Undo, and Redo. In Excel 2007 the Web toolbar from previous versions is gone, so you have to add Web tools to the Quick Access Toolbar to perform many Web-related actions.

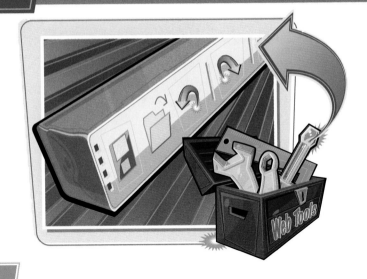

Add Web Tools to the Quick Access Toolbar

1. Click the **Office** button (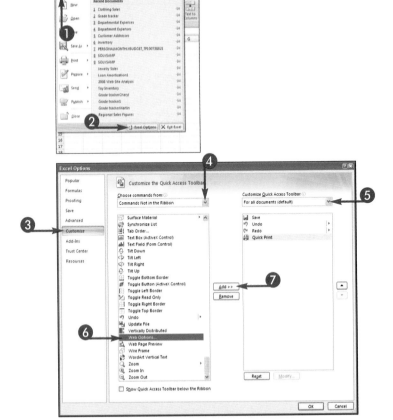).

2. Click **Excel Options**.

3. Click **Customization**.

4. Click here to select the Commands Not in the Ribbon category of commands.

5. Click here to specify whether changes are only for this document or for all documents.

6. Click a Web command, such as **Save as Web Page**, **Publish as Web Page**, **Web Page Preview**, or **Web Options**.

7. Click **Add**.

8. Repeat steps **6** and **7** to add all Web commands.

● The commands appear in the list of Quick Access commands.

⑨ Click these arrows to move commands up or down in the list.

⑩ Click **OK** to save your changes.

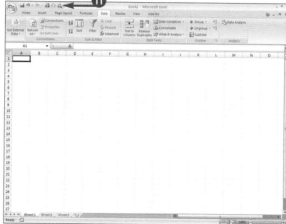

⑪ Click any tool to use a Quick Access command.

TIPS

Can I get back to the original Quick Access Toolbar settings?

Yes. In the Customize area of Excel Options, click **Reset**. Any commands you have added are removed. Click **OK** to save the changes.

Is there a quicker way to add or remove a tool to the Quick Access Toolbar?

Yes, but only if the tool exists on the Ribbon. Right-click any tool on the Ribbon and choose **Add to Quick Access Toolbar**. To remove a tool on the toolbar, right-click it and choose **Remove from Quick Access Toolbar**.

Publish a Workbook as a Web Page

You can turn an Excel workbook into an HTML file that you can publish on the Web. When you activate the Publish as Web page command, Excel creates a file containing all the necessary HTML coding required to generate a Web page that can be read by Web browsers.

You can save the entire workbook as a Web page, a sheet, or a range of cells on a worksheet. If your workbook consists of only one worksheet, the HTML file you create contains only the single sheet.

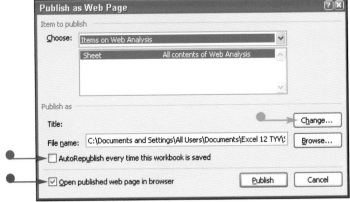

Publish a Workbook as a Web Page

① Click **Publish as Web Page** (🔳) on the Quick Access toolbar.

The Publish as Web Page dialog box appears.

② Choose any of the following settings:

● Click **Change** to display a dialog box where you can specify a title for the page.

● Click here to set the workbook to publish to the Web each time you save it.

● Click here to open the workbook as a Web preview in a browser after you publish it.

3 Click the **Choose** ▼ to select what portion of the workbook you want to publish.

4 Click **Browse** and specify a server path and filename.

5 Click **Publish**.

Excel saves the file as a Web page.

● The file opens as a preview in your browser, assuming you selected that option.

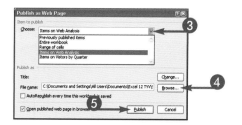

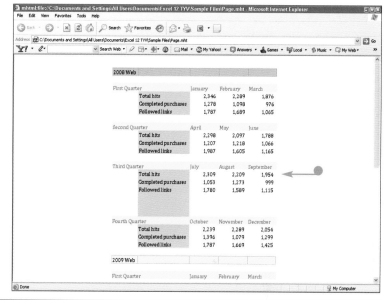

Can I preview my file as a Web page before I publish it?

Yes, you can. Just follow these steps:

1 Click **Web Page Preview** (⊞) on the Quick Access Toolbar.

Your default Web browser opens and displays the worksheet as a Web page.

2 Click the **Close** button (☒) to close the browser window and return to Excel.

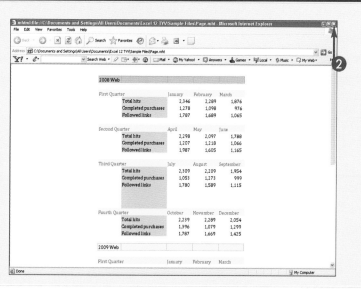

Insert a Hyperlink

You can insert hyperlinks into your worksheets that, when clicked, open a Web page. When linking to a Web page you must designate the *URL*, which stands for Uniform Resource Locator, the unique address that identifies the Web page.

You can also use hyperlinks to link to other files on your computer. You must designate the address or path of the page you want to link to when adding links to a worksheet.

Insert a Hyperlink

1 Select the text or image you want to use as a hyperlink.

2 Click the **Insert** tab.

3 Click **Hyperlink**.

The Insert Hyperlink dialog box appears.

4 Click the type of document to which you want to link.

5 Select the page or type the address (URL) of the page to which you want to link.

● To browse the Internet to look for the page, you can click the **Browse the Web** (🔍) button and open your default browser window.

6 Click **OK**.

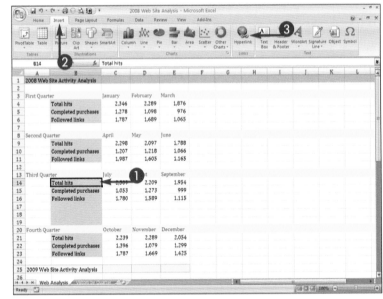

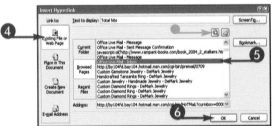

Excel creates a hyperlink and closes the dialog box.

7 While holding down **Ctrl**, click the link to test it.

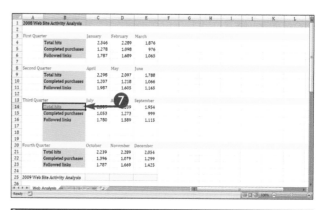

● The default Web browser opens and displays the designated page.

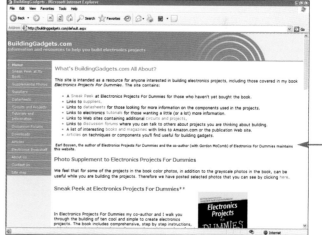

TIPS

How do I edit a link?

To change a link, such as to edit the Web page URL, you can reopen the Edit Hyperlink dialog box and make any necessary changes. Right-click the link and click **Edit Hyperlink**. The Edit Hyperlink dialog box appears. You can use the dialog box to change the hyperlink text, address, or the type of page you want to use in the link.

How do I remove a hyperlink from my worksheet?

You can right-click a link and click **Remove Hyperlink** from the shortcut menu. Excel removes the associated link and leaves the text or image. To remove a hyperlink from the Edit Hyperlink dialog box, you can click **Remove Link**.

Download a Stock Quote

You can download current stock quotes from the Web and insert them into your Excel worksheets. You can use your Internet connection and Excel's Research task pane to look up stock quotes online.

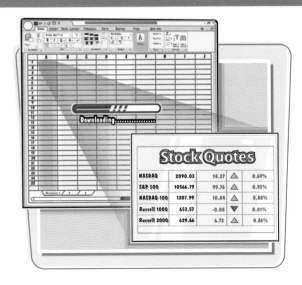

Download a Stock Quote

① Click a cell that will hold the stock quote.

② Click the **Review** tab.

③ Click **Research**.

Note: To learn more about Excel's task panes, see Chapter 1.

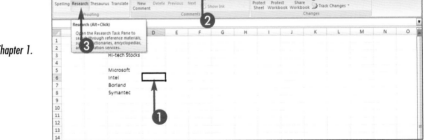

The Research task pane opens.

④ Click the ▾.

⑤ Click **MSN Money Stock Quotes**.

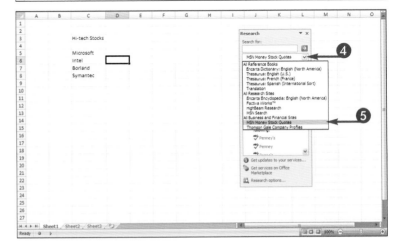

⑥ Type the stock ticker for the stock you want to look up.

⑦ Click **Start Searching** ().

● The Research pane displays the results.

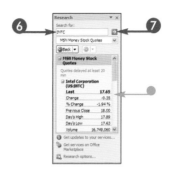

⑧ Click **Insert Price**.

You may have to scroll down in the Results pane to access the Insert Price button.

● Excel inserts the current quote into the cell.

● You can click the Research task pane's **Close** button (✕).

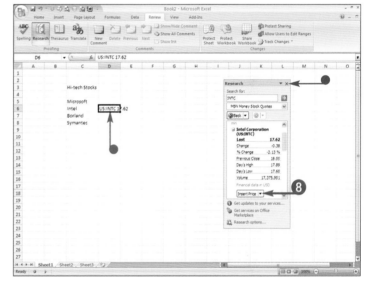

TIPS

How can I view more information about a particular stock?

You can click the **Detailed Quote** link under the More on MSN Money heading in the Research task pane to open the MSN Web site and view more detailed information about a stock. You might have to scroll down a bit to locate the link. When you click the link, your default Web browser opens and displays the information along with the Research task pane.

What else can I do with the Research task pane?

You can also use the Research task pane to look up and translate words. For example, the thesaurus helps you to look up similar words, and the Encarta Encyclopedia allows you to look up topics of interest. You can use the translation features to translate words into other languages, which is useful if you share worksheets with users in other countries. To learn more about how task panes work in Excel, see Chapter 1.

Copy Web Data to a Worksheet

You can copy data from a Web page and insert that data into your worksheet cells. For example, you might gather information pertaining to your company to include in a financial worksheet.

You must be connected to the Internet to copy data from Web pages. Make sure you obtain appropriate permission to use data you copy from someone's Web site.

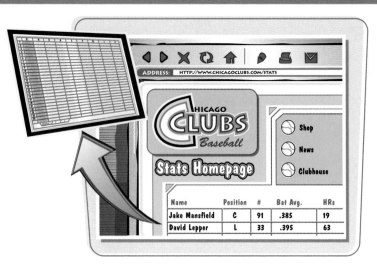

Copy Web Data to a Worksheet

① Use your Web browser to view the page containing the data you want to copy.

② Select the data you want to copy.

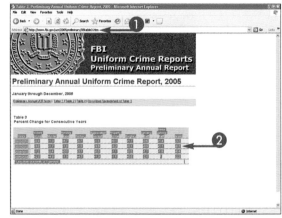

③ Click **Edit**.

④ Click **Copy**.

You can also press `Ctrl` + `C` to copy selected data to the Windows Clipboard.

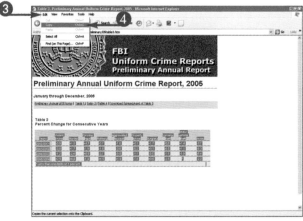

⑤ Open the worksheet that contains the cell or cells where you want to paste the copied data.

⑥ Click in the cell or cells where you want to paste the data.

⑦ Click the **Home** tab.

⑧ Click **Paste**.

You can also press Ctrl + V to paste data.

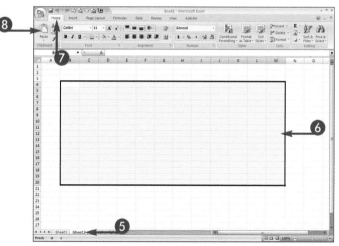

● Excel pastes the data into the worksheet.

● If the **Paste Options smart tag** icon appears, you can click the icon (🖹) to view additional paste options you can apply.

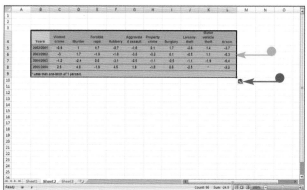

TIPS

Can I drag and drop data from a Web page into a worksheet?

Yes. If you display both the browser window and the Excel window at the same time, you can drag data from the Web page into your worksheet cells. To resize a program window, position the mouse pointer over the edge of the window and then click and drag to resize the window. To return the window to full size again, click the **Maximize** icon (🗖).

What types of Web data are suitable for copying into Excel?

You can copy any type of data to place in a worksheet cell. For example, you might copy a text quote or an image. Web page table data also copies easily into Excel's grid format. After you copy the data into a worksheet, you might need to apply some formatting commands to make the data more presentable.

Run a Web Query

You can run a Web query to import data from the Internet to use in your worksheets. A *query* is an action that retrieves data for analysis in Excel.

You must be connected to the Internet to perform a Web query. Make sure you obtain appropriate permission any time you copy data from someone's Web site.

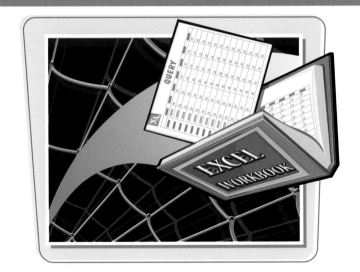

Run a Query

1. Click the **Data** tab.

2. Click **Get External Data**.

3. Click **From Web**.

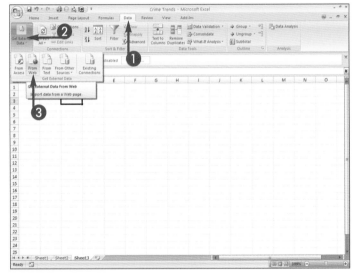

The New Web Query dialog box opens and displays your default browser home page.

4. Type the URL for the Web site you want to query.

5. Click **Go** or press Enter.

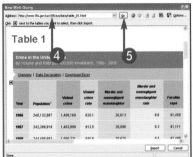

The New Web Query dialog box displays the page.

⑥ Click ➡ next to the table you want to select.

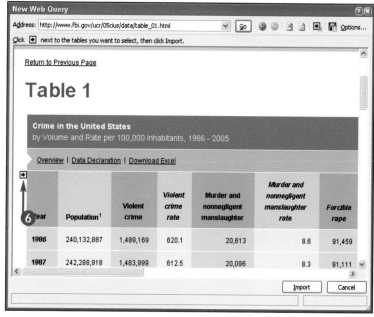

The Import Data dialog box appears.

⑦ Click 🔳 to choose the cells where you want to place the imported data.

⑧ Designate where you want to insert the imported data (○ changes to ⦿).

⑨ Click OK.

How do I control what formatting is imported?

You can use the Import Data dialog box to determine what formatting and other import settings are assigned to the data. When viewing the Import Data dialog box, follow these steps to set any additional options:

① Click **Properties**.

The External Data Range Properties dialog box opens.

② Click any data formatting and layout options you want to apply to the data you import (☐ changes to ☑ or ○ changes to ⦿).

③ Click **OK**.

Excel returns you to the New Web Query dialog box to finish importing the data.

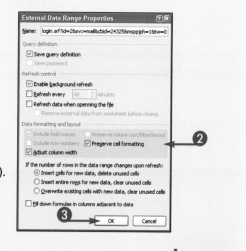

continued

After you run a Web query, you can perform all kinds of analyses on the data you import, such as creating new formulas, changing the existing values, and so on. You can save the query to use again at a later time. Queries are saved with the .iqy file extension. By default, Excel saves queries to the Queries folder unless specified otherwise.

Run a Web Query (continued)

You can import the data into the existing worksheet or import the data onto a new sheet.

⑩ Click 🔳 again.

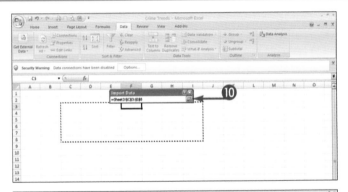

● Excel imports the data.

You can make changes to the data to perform your own analysis, such as changing data and creating your own formulas.

● Any time you want to refresh external data, click **Data** and then click **Refresh All**.

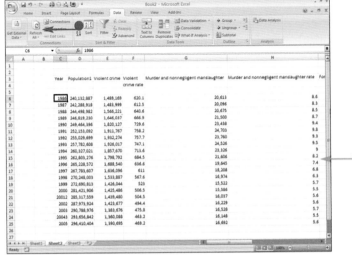

Save a Query

① Right-click anywhere in the query results and choose **Edit Query**.

The Edit Web Query dialog box opens.

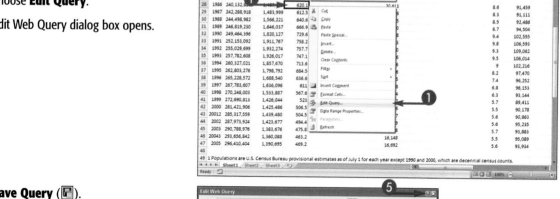

② Click **Save Query** (🖫).

The Save As dialog box opens.

③ Type a name for the query.

④ Click **Save**.

Excel saves the query.

⑤ Click 🖳 in the Edit Web Query dialog box to close it.

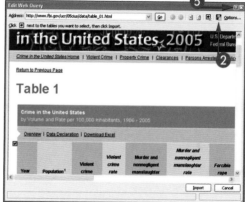

How do I use the same query in another workbook?

After you save a query, you can access it again with other Excel files. Follow these steps:

① Follow the steps in this section to create and save a query.

② Click **Data**.

③ Click **From Other Sources**.

④ Click **Microsoft Queries**.

The Choose Data Source dialog box appears.

⑤ Click the **Queries** tab.

⑥ Double-click the saved query you want to run.

Excel runs the saved query.

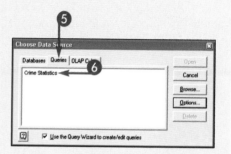

CHAPTER 5

Improving Excel Efficiency

You can improve the way you use Excel by tapping into its many customizing features and tools. This chapter shows you how to change the appearance of program elements, control default file locations, activate speech commands, work with macros, and create templates.

Personalize the Excel Program Window

You can personalize the Excel program window to look the way you want. For example, you might want to enable or disable Live Preview, or choose to show or hide enhanced ScreenTips. The Excel Options Popular dialog box offers all kinds of options for customizing Excel.

Personalize the Excel Program Window

① Click the **Office** button (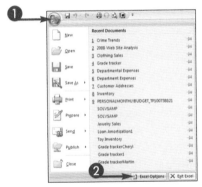).

② Click **Excel Options**.

The **Excel Options** window opens.

③ Click **Popular**.

④ Set any options you want to turn on or off.

● Click here (☑ changes to ☐) to turn off the display of the Mini Toolbar that appears when working with text.

● Click the **Screen Tip Scheme** ▼ and select **Don't Show Enhanced ScreenTips** to turn off this feature.

● Click here (☑ changes to ☐) to disable Live Preview, which previews choices you make in galleries before you apply them.

● Click **Color Scheme** ▼ to choose a different Color Scheme.

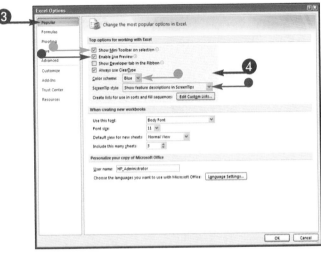

● Click **Default View For New Sheets** 🔽
to choose a different default view for
worksheets.

⑤ Click **OK**.

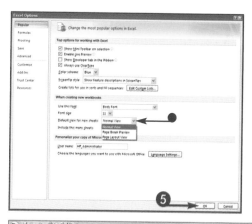

Excel applies any changes you made to the
program window.

● In this example, the Enhanced ScreenTips
are hidden and a different color scheme
has been applied.

TIPS

Can I modify what is displayed on the Ribbon?

No. The only tool buttons you can modify are
those used on the Quick Access
Toolbar. To do that you make
changes in the Customize
portion of the
Excel Options.
See Chapter 1
for more about
setting up the
Quick Access
Toolbar.

Can I stop gridlines from displaying?

Yes. You can do this from
two places on the
Ribbon: The Page
Layout and the View
tabs. Each has a
check box you can click
(☑ changes to ☐) to
turn gridlines off. Click
this check box again
(☐ changes to ☑) to turn
them on again.

Change the Default Font

By default, Excel assigns Calibri, 11 point as the font and font size in every new workbook you open. Any data you type into the worksheet cells uses the default settings. If you prefer a different font and size, you can designate another choice using the Excel Options, Personalize dialog box. For example, you might want to assign a larger font size to make your worksheet data easier to read.

Change the Default Font

① Click ▣.

② Click **Excel Options**.

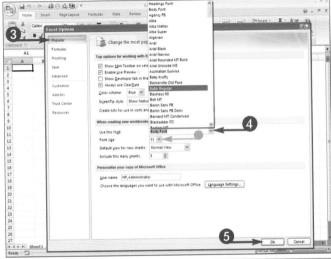

The Excel Options window opens.

③ Click **Popular**.

④ Click here and then click a font.

● You can change the default font size here.

⑤ Click **OK**.

A dialog box appears instructing you to quit and restart Excel for your changes to take effect. Click **OK**. The new font appears as an option when you restart Excel.

By default, Excel's Open and Save As dialog boxes are automatically set up to display and store your files in the My Documents folder. You might prefer to keep your workbooks in a different folder. You can specify another folder as the default folder and save yourself time otherwise spent navigating to the folder containing your Excel files.

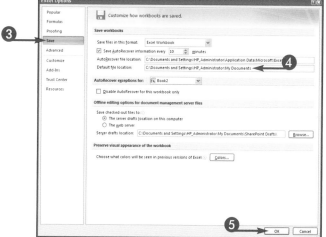

Change the Default File Location

1 Click 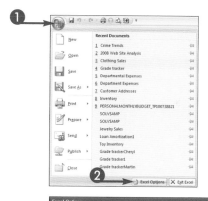.

2 Click **Excel Options**.

The Excel Options window opens.

3 Click **Save**.

4 Click inside the Default file location box and then type the new path to the location where you want to save your Excel files.

5 Click **OK** to apply the changes.

Open Files in a Specified Folder Automatically

If you find yourself using the same workbooks over and over again, you can tell Excel to open files in a designated folder automatically whenever you open Excel.

① Click .

② Click **Excel Options**.

The Excel Options window opens.

③ Click **Advanced**.

You might have to scroll down until you see the General group of commands.

④ Type the full path to the folder you want to open.

⑤ Click **OK** to apply the changes.

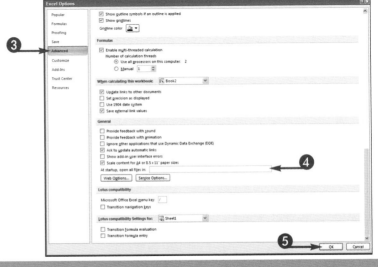

Set Macro Security

A *macro* is an automatically executable series of keystrokes that perform some action. Some macros may run when you start an Excel file, to enable certain automatic functions you need. Other macros can execute viruses or change data in your worksheet in ways you do not expect. You can set up macro security to run macros in the way that you choose.

Set Macro Security

① Click 🖫.

② Click **Excel Options**.

③ Click **Trust Center**.

④ Click **Trust Center Settings**.

The Trust Center dialog box opens.

⑤ Click **Macro Settings**.

⑥ Click an option to make settings (○ changes to ◉).

⑦ Click **OK**.

You can use macros to automate the tasks you perform in Excel. For example, you can create a macro to apply formatting, assign a formula, or print sheets. After you record a macro, Excel saves the actions so you can reuse the macro.

You can assign a keyboard shortcut key to your macro and activate the macro at any time using the keyboard. A shortcut key typically involves two keyboard keys pressed in combination.

Record a Macro

1 To access Macro tools, first display the Developer tab (this setting is in the Popular section of Excel Options).

2 Click the **Developer** tab.

3 Click **Record Macro**.

The Record Macro dialog box opens.

4 Type a name for the macro.

Note: Macro names have to start with a letter or underscore and can contain no spaces.

5 Assign a shortcut key for the macro if you wish.

A shortcut key is a combination of two keyboard keys you can use to activate a command.

● You can click here to store the macro in a workbook other than the default location.

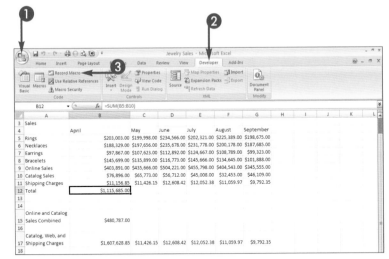

● Optionally, you can type a description of the macro here.

⑥ Click **OK**.

The Record Macro button on the Developer tab of the Ribbon changes to the Stop Recording button.

⑦ Execute each command or task you want to record as a macro.

⑧ When finished, click the **Stop Recording** button (☐).

Excel saves your actions.

To execute the macro at any time, press the keyboard shortcut you assigned, such as Ctrl + T .

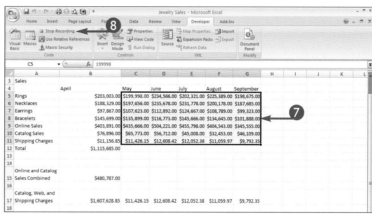

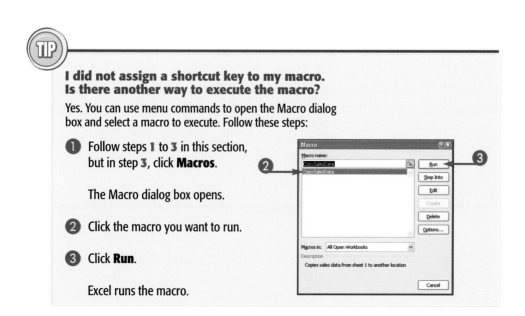

TIP

I did not assign a shortcut key to my macro. Is there another way to execute the macro?

Yes. You can use menu commands to open the Macro dialog box and select a macro to execute. Follow these steps:

① Follow steps **1** to **3** in this section, but in step **3**, click **Macros**.

The Macro dialog box opens.

② Click the macro you want to run.

③ Click **Run**.

Excel runs the macro.

Create an Excel Template

If you find yourself using the same formatting and worksheet elements over and over again, you can turn the information into a template file to reuse with other workbooks. For example, you can create templates for specific tasks and projects. Templates include formatting, styles, and standardized data, such as text labels and formulas.

You can store your templates in the Templates folder for handy application later.

Create an Excel Template

① Create a workbook containing all the elements and formatting you want to use as a template.

To create a worksheet template, create a workbook with only one sheet.

② Click 🔘.

③ Click **Save As**.

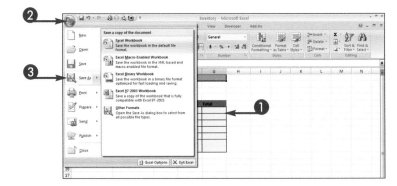

The Save As dialog box opens.

④ Click the **Save as type** 🔽.

⑤ Click **Excel Template**.

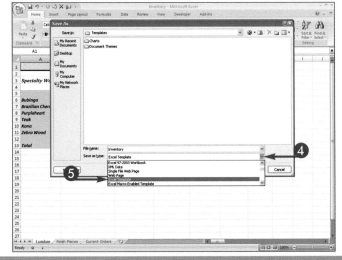

6 Navigate to the folder in which you want to store the template.

To keep your templates manageable, store them in the default Templates folder, which appears automatically when you activate the Template file type.

7 Type a filename for the template.

8 Click **Save**.

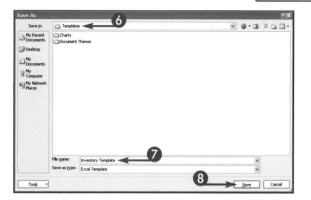

Excel saves the template file.

● The .xlt extension is added to the file, and the new filename appears in the Title bar.

Note: *See the next section to learn how to apply an Excel template.*

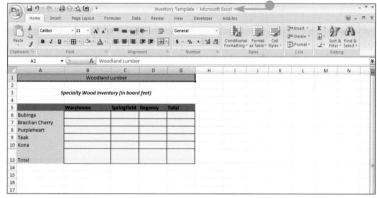

Can I store my templates in a different folder?

Yes. However, the default Templates folder works best for templates you want to access through Excel's Templates dialog box. Any template you place in the default Templates folder appears listed in the Templates dialog box. The full path to the Templates folder is C:\Documents and Settings\user_name\ Application Data\ Microsoft\Templates (substitute your user name for "user_name" in the path). To learn more about applying templates, see the next section, "Apply an Excel Template."

What types of templates can I create for Excel?

Your templates can focus on any project or task you want. For example, you might create a template for entering quarterly sales data or a template for ordering inventory. Regardless of the focus of the template, you can create either a workbook template, which contains several sheets, or a worksheet template, which contains preset data for a single sheet.

Apply an Excel Template

You can use Excel templates to speed up your workbook creation. *Templates* are ready-made documents you can use to quickly assemble spreadsheets. Excel includes several premade templates that contain preformatted placeholder text; all you have to do is add your own text. You can also apply any templates you create for your own work use.

① Click .

② Click **New**.

The New Workbook window opens.

③ Click **My templates**.

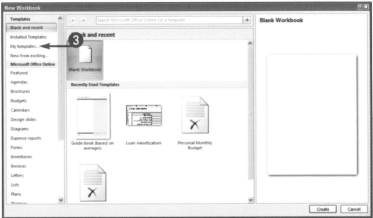

The New dialog box opens. Excel displays any saved templates you created and saved to the Templates folder.

④ Click the template you want to open.

⑤ Click **OK**.

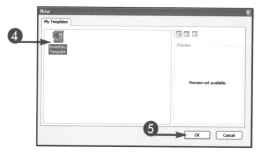

● Excel opens the template file, adding a numeral to the filename (for example, Inventory Template1).

You can make changes to the data and formatting as needed.

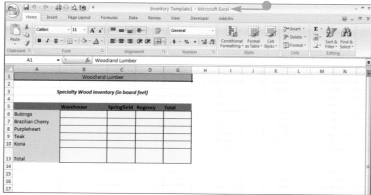

TIPS

Where can I find more Excel templates?

You can click any of the categories in the Microsoft Office Online listing in the New Workbook dialog box. Your computer will connect to the Internet and display available templates in that category.

What premade templates install with Excel?

You can find 13 premade templates by clicking the Installed Templates link in the New Workbook dialog box, including Balance Sheet, Billing Statement, Expense Statement, General Ledger, Loan Amortization, Sales Invoice, and Timecard. The template names describe the focus of each template. You can customize each template by making your own changes to the formatting and data after opening the template file, and then save the changes as a new template. See the previous section to learn how to create template files in Excel.

Index

Numbers and Symbols

3-D charts
>   manipulate, 186–187
>   reset, 187

3-D effects, objects, 159
+ (addition) operator, 67
/ (division) operator, 67
= (equal to) operator, 67
^ (exponentiation) operator, 67
> (greater than) operator, 67
< (less than) operator, 67
* (multiplication) operator, 67
<> (not equal to) operator, 67
% (percentage) operator, 67
- (subtraction) operator, 67

A

absolute cell references, 70–71
absolute formulas, copy, 73
Accept or Reject Changes dialog box, 248
Accounting format, 119
active cell, 53
active worksheet, 9, 54
add-ins, load, 222–223
Add-Ins dialog box, 223
alignment
>   horizontal, 124
>   justified, 125
>   vertical, 125

Alignment dialog box, 126
AND function, 79
apply functions, 80–83
area charts, 179
arguments, functions, 78
arrange windows, 28–29
Arrange Windows dialog box, 28–29
auditing worksheets for errors, 88–89
AutoCorrect, add misspelling, 44–45
AutoCorrect dialog box, 45
AutoFill
>   custom list, 43
>   number series, 43
>   text series, 42

AutoFill Options smart tag, 73
AutoFilter, database data, 212–213
AutoFooter, 166–167
AutoHeader, 166–167
AutoSum, 84–85
AVERAGE function, 79
axes, charts, 185

B

background
>   cells, color, 130–131
>   worksheets, 132

bar charts, 179
bold text, 114–115
borders
>   color, 129
>   custom, 129
>   Quick Borders, 128

Borders icon, 128
Bottom Align icon, 125
bubble charts, 179
built-in functions, 81

C

cascaded windows, 28
category axis, charts, 179
cell addresses, 52
cell ranges. *See* ranges
cell references
>   absolute, 70
>   description, 66
>   error checking, 86
>   formulas and, 68
>   mixed, 71

>   from other worksheets, 77
>   relative, 70, 71

cells
>   active, 53, 54
>   AutoSum and, 84–85
>   color, background, 130–131
>   column, select, 41
>   delete, 96
>   description, 52
>   formatting, remove, 97
>   name, 74
>   row, select, 41
>   select, 40–41
>   totalling, 84–85
>   type into, 36
>   Watch Window, 221

center, data across columns, 102
Center icon, 124
Change Chart Type dialog box, 184
changes in workbook, track and review, 246–249
Chart Layouts, 192
chart title, charts, 179
charts
>   3-D, 186–187
>   area, 179
>   axes, titles, 185
>   bar, 179
>   bubble, 179
>   category axis, 179
>   category axis title, 179
>   column, 179
>   create, 180–181
>   customize, 178
>   data, change, 191
>   data series, 178, 179
>   default, 181
>   doughnut, 179
>   format, Chart Layouts, 192
>   galleries, 180–181
>   legend, 179
>   line, 179
>   move, 182
>   move, to different worksheet, 183
>   noncontiguous data, 181
>   objects, format, 188–189
>   objects, insert, 190
>   pie, 179
>   plot area, 179
>   print, 189
>   radar, 179
>   resize, 183
>   scatter, 179
>   SmartArt, 193
>   stock, 179
>   styles, 192
>   surface, 179
>   text font, 189
>   title, 179
>   type, change, 184
>   value axis, 179
>   value axis title, 179

Charts group, galleries, 180
clip art
>   copy between collections, 145
>   details about, 143
>   download from Web, 146–147
>   insert, 142–143
>   search for, 143
>   view, 144–145

Clip Art task pane, 142–143
Clip Organizer, 144–145
close
>   Excel, 7
>   workbooks, 26

color
>   borders, 129
>   cell background, 130–131
>   font, 121

Index

Index

Index